W9-BWL-119

RICHARD & ELIZABETH ADLER

Needlepoint

— A NEW LOOK —

RICHARD & ELIZABETH ADLER

Needlepoint
—— A NEW LOOK ——

SIDGWICK & JACKSON

LONDON

First published in Great Britain in 1981 by
Sidgwick & Jackson Limited

Reprinted December 1981
Reprinted July 1984

Copyright © Elizabeth and Richard Adler 1981

Photography by Ian O'Leary
Cover and book design by Andy Pittaway
Finished artwork for cover, stitch and chart
diagrams by Walkaways Limited
Finished artwork for text pages by Fieldway Press
Limited

ISBN 0-283-98797-9 (hardcover)
ISBN 0-283-98936-X (softcover)

Printed in Great Britain by
The Garden City Press Limited
Letchworth, Hertfordshire
for Sidgwick & Jackson Limited
1 Tavistock Chambers, Bloomsbury Way
London WC1A 2SG

We should like to give our sincere thanks to: Janey Morris; Margaret Willes, our editor; Andy Pittaway, Randy Weeks and Pete Dent at Walkaways; Ian O'Leary and Barbara Minter. All the designs were created and worked by Richard and Elizabeth Adler, except for the Beaded Frame, which was worked by Diana Keay.

To Anabelle with Love

CONTENTS

INTRODUCTION

$\mathcal{N}$eedlepoint is fascinating. The process of setting stitch after stitch in place is wonderfully soothing; choosing the next stitch, the next colour, working through a design (particularly if it is *your* design) is creatively satisfying. There is great pleasure to be found in watching a piece of work emerge in your hands through the soothing rhythm of stitching. No wonder then, in this modern world, that needlepoint is becoming so popular. Film stars do it during the interminable waits on set, businessmen can be seen stitching away on aeroplanes, secretaries work at it in their lunch hours.

So this book is for contemporary men and women who are interested in needlepoint, whether they are beginners or not. And of course it is for children too, the needle artists of the future. It is for people like us, with busy lives and time-consuming jobs, with children to look after, school holidays and dinner parties to organize, and homes that we enjoy filling with pretty things. We do not conform to that well-worn image of little old ladies working away at fire-screens or spectacle cases. We are business people, doctors and decorators, actors, farmers, publicans and publishers – real people in a real world.

What we will teach you in this book is relevant to today, and is not obscured by all kinds of ideas about what 'should be' because it 'always has been'.

*'Others think that if the work be in
"dowdy" colours it may pass under the sacred
name of ART . . .'*

wrote Elizabeth Glaister in 1880, and her words still apply today. So no more dreary, derivative little patterns in porridgy colours.

Instead, we will show you how to design and work for yourself whatever *you* want. We will show you how to use colour gracefully and with delicacy, and how to relate it to your surroundings. This book is unlike any other needlepoint primer because there are no rules, no 'musts' and above all no patterns to be copied (although everything you need to know is included if you feel that you *must* copy). What we are about to do is get you started on a piece of needlepoint that you will design yourself. It is your personal taste that will make it live.

We hope that our methods will point the way to a new creative freedom. First of all, to develop any skill whether it is cooking a good meal or playing tennis, you must be familiar with the basic techniques. For needlepoint, you will find everything that you need to know here. In the appropriate chapters we will discuss types and weights of canvas, examine the tempting range of threads now on the market, provide easy-to-follow stitch diagrams and ways of transferring your designs to your canvas – all with the minimum of fuss and formality. But if, armed with all this new information and ready to set the first stitch, your mind is a creative blank, we'll help to answer the question 'what shall I *do?*'

What has to be overcome is awe of the magic words 'design' and 'inspiration'. The world is full of patterns and images that can be adapted, and we are all surrounded by a wealth of stimuli. We once made a series of doorstops with a difference – emblazoned with *The Times*, Harrods and Pepsi logos (see pages 110–111). A direct steal in true design terms, but made our own in the way we chose to adapt them.

Every home is a kaleidoscope of colour and pattern, in carpets, commercial packagings, wallpapers and fabrics. We all have highly developed personal preferences, reflected in the clothes and furnishings we choose to surround ourselves with. Your needlework should be a distillation of your own taste. If you begin by looking around you, and choose the simplest and strongest influences from familiar surroundings, you will soon gain the confidence to look further afield for inspiration, and to experiment more widely. At the same time you will be learning practical things like how to use particular stitches within your design, how to use the different textures of threads and how to use colour within the limitations of your small piece of canvas.

For example, we have a sofa in our studio, upholstered in a bold pattern with a large motif. We wanted to make some cushions for it, but we certainly didn't want boring old plain ones. The answer was to use the fabric as a design source for three cushions, to complement the fabric without just replicating the pattern. We took the pattern and concentrated on the less strong elements in it, picking out the beautiful colours to echo in stitchery. A solution like this can be as easy or challenging as you like.

One of our cushions adopts just one simple motif, shades of two main fabric colours in only one thread texture, and two stitches. Another takes the main flower design from the fabric, works it in several shades and different yarns, and five stitches, setting the whole design in an interesting octagonal border. The third cushion takes the bamboo border pattern of the fabric, but uses it as a central panel. The design is quite complex in its use of stitches, colours and textures. To give you a much more detailed idea of how adaptation like this is done in practical terms, pictures of the fabric and cushions, and working details for each one, are given on pages 64–73.

The general lesson, then, is to take a familiar and well-loved pattern and be as restrained or ambitious as you like in adapting it. One of the joys of it all is that you have the reference right there in front of you, so that you can see as you go along whether you are choosing the right shades, whether you have got the size right, that you are not becoming too over-ornamental. You are not grappling with some shifting, abstract ideal inside your own head. And, of course, your finished piece of work will be unique as well as the perfect complement for your favourite chair.

You may be thinking now that it is going to be a long time before you can put any of this theory properly into practice. In fact, it is all quite straightforward and simple, and the next step is to show you how to begin. If you are a complete novice, look at the first easy project set out on pages 41–50. You need only learn one stitch, you will be working with shades of only one colour, and the project itself – to make a design around an initial – is personal, and *small enough to finish quickly*. In the early stages, what you need is results. If you are not an absolute beginner, of course, just turn to the later chapters for something more challenging.

Before you begin, however, be warned. Once you start doing needlepoint, it's difficult to put it down. Enthusiasts are always looking forward to putting in the next bit of the design, 'just wanting to get this flower finished', planning the next project. It can become totally absorbing, in the most beneficial way. And, of course, one of its great advantages is that it is so portable. Just roll it up and take it with you, on the train or plane, to work or on holiday to do by the pool. Even if you only have time to put in a dozen stitches, the sense of tranquillity it brings is still there.

Finally, the word 'needlepoint' itself. Historically, needlepoint referred to needlepoint lace, something entirely different. The word's contemporary usage, however, which has come to us from the USA, means the type of canvas work that you see in this book. We are not doing 'tapestry' (which also historically meant something else), or 'canvas embroidery', which drab phrase seems to belong to Victorian times. We are doing needlepoint.

MATERIALS

The combination of various wools and threads
gives your design its texture. What follows is a
brief description of the qualities of each of the
readily available varieties.

TAPESTRY WOOL

A British wool which comes in a good range of traditional tapestry colours, and is used straight from the skein. It is a firmly twisted single strand wool and will not cover all the different mesh sizes of canvas, but it is perfect for no. 12 single mesh and no. 10 double mesh (or Penelope) canvas. See pages 18–19 for a description of the various types of canvas.

STRANDABLE WOOL

This 3-ply strandable wool is one of the best for needlepoint, mainly because of its versatility. When it is separated and used as a single strand, it is suitable for use on a fine no. 18 canvas, or up to the even finer 22 mesh. If it is worked as two strands, it is suitable for nos 12 and 14, varying a little according to stitch tension and the type of stitch being used. Two strands are more usual for no. 16 canvas. Used in the full 3-ply strand, it is suitable for a no. 10 canvas which would normally be used for a rug or where a strong and hard-wearing surface is necessary.

This is the general rule, but of course we all have different tension in our stitches, so you may need to adjust these guidelines a little if you have trouble pulling the strands through the canvas. The colours of strandable wool are particularly lovely and beautifully shaded.

PERLÉ

This thread has a twisted silken appearance and a very soft shine. It comes in a beautiful range of shaded colours which are very easy to incorporate into your colour scheme. It is available in two thicknesses, no. 3 and no. 5. Number 5 is slightly thinner than no. 3 and is most suitable for use on a no. 14 or 16 mesh canvas, while no. 3 can be used on no. 14 canvas and on any of the larger meshes. We prefer to use perlé in place of gold thread which we feel can be too dominating in a piece of needlepoint, and is difficult to incorporate in the average design as it is really more suited to ecclesiastical surroundings. Unless you really need a very strong effect, try using the softer glow of a perlé in a gold shade instead.

STRANDED COTTON
(sometimes called 'floss' or 'silk')
This thread has a high gloss and a smooth texture which is composed of seven strands which can be separated for use on different sizes of canvas as required. Care should be taken when pulling this thread through the canvas though, as one strand may not pull through as evenly as its fellows, leaving a loop on the surface of your work. It is worth the trouble to use, however, as it does have such a dramatic effect and puts a lovely shine where you need a highlight. It contrasts splendidly with the matte texture of the wools.

SOFT EMBROIDERY COTTON
A matte cotton thread with a flat, unreflecting surface when stitched. It provides an excellent contrast with the softness of the wools and the shine of the perlés and stranded cottons. It is best in the more subtle colours.

OTHER THREADS
We are constantly discovering more and more different threads and yarns. There are mixtures of silk and linen, nubby-textured wools, raw linen, chenilles, and opalescent thread which has great delicacy when used for outlining or highlighting. There is even a velvet thread which looks a little like pipe cleaners until you use it, then it gives a beautifully soft velvety appearance and is especially effective on raised-textured stitches.

Pure silk thread is so beautiful, but care must be taken as the dyes on some of the colours are not always fast and therefore should be avoided for work which has to be wet or dampened to be stretched. It has the same tendency to pull as the stranded cotton and the same care must be taken when using it, and for these reasons we recommend using stranded cotton instead wherever possible, rather than the silk. It is excellent however used in pictorial designs for flesh colours, or highlights, as the colours are very subtle and there is a vast colour range.

These lovely threads are all for your future use, but sadly they can be quite expensive and not all are easy to find. When you do come across new and different threads on your travels it is well worth picking some up to bring back with you.

17

CANVAS

We recommend that you use *single mesh canvas,* for the simple reason that it is easier to see where the holes are. Unless you really need to use the double mesh (Penelope) canvas we see no reason to distract the eye with a double line of threads – which can create a problem for the contact-lensed, or other near-sighted people. If you intend to explore the intricacies of 'petit-point', however, double mesh is the canvas to use. There is also now an Interlock (Leno) canvas on the market in single mesh.

If you are working in pale colours it is better to use white canvas, but brown or ecru are also readily available colours.

The single mesh canvas (known as mono-canvas) comes in different sizes – or meshes – that relate to the number of threads to the inch. Number 10 canvas, therefore, has 100 threads to the square inch and no. 12 has 144 threads to the square inch. If you were working tent or diagonal tent stitch each thread would represent a stitch, therefore there are 100 stitches to the square inch on no. 10 canvas, and 144 stitches to the square inch on no. 12, and so on.

Good canvas has no flaws in it, no lumps or knots. It has highly polished smooth threads (and this is important, because otherwise it will snag your wools and silks), and will be crisp and firm to the touch. In fact it will feel stiff and almost intractable at first, but don't worry – you can roll it up, fold it, curl it up or just scrunch it. When it is finished and has been dampened and stretched it will all spring back into place and will be as smooth and crisp as when you started.

Most canvas is sold by the metre, and usually half a metre is the minimum amount sold. From a piece of this size you can usually get two working canvases.

The edges of the canvas must be bound before work is started to prevent the annoying fraying that inevitably happens otherwise. You can lose quite a few inches of canvas this way, strand by strand, to say nothing of the loose threads which can get caught up in your stitches, so it is worth the effort. (See the chapter on techniques for how to bind your canvas.)

We recommend a no. 14 mesh canvas for beginners. It is fine enough for detail and delicacy without being too taxing on the eyes or too time-consuming to 'fill'. For children we recommend a no. 12 canvas as they need the gratification of quicker results. Go on to no. 16 when you feel the need for rather finer work (most of the designs in this book were worked on no. 16 mesh canvas). Number 18 is the canvas for very delicate things with a lot of detail like samplers, or perhaps cushions for a 'boudoir' decorated with lace or broderie anglaise around the edges. The 'lace' cushion on page 92 was worked on no. 18 canvas. Number 10 canvas is recommended for rugs or where a heavier wool is used for a hard-wearing surface.

NEEDLES
Tapestry needles are available in most high street shops. For a no. 14 canvas you will need a no. 18 needle; for a no. 16 canvas use a no. 20 needle; for a no. 18 canvas use a no. 22 needle; and for a no. 10 canvas use a no. 18 needle.

Remember that the colours, the wools and different textures of the threads, the canvas and the needles are only the ingredients. Your design is the recipe which brings them all together.

SCISSORS
You must have a pair of scissors with sharp points. The points are essential for unpicking stitches – unfortunately something that happens to us all in needlepoint. In fact, when in any doubt at all about the success of a colour or a stitch, take it out. If you are not happy with it right away then something is wrong, and you will still be unhappy with it when you are finished. So a good pair of scissors is vital, with a sharp point to help you to slide the scissors under the stitch without catching and cutting the canvas. Take care when unpicking. We have used an old pair of nail scissors for years and despite more elaborate later purchases they are still the pair we are most comfortable with. So, the fancier models you see around may not necessarily be the best for your purpose.

FRAMES
The use of a frame is a personal thing, but it is not really necessary for the sort of needlepoint we are doing in this book. We never use one,

preferring to feel the flexibility of the canvas and enjoying the speed of working with it like this. Working with a frame is slower and more limiting. We would use a frame only for a very large piece of work where it is likely to become very heavy. However, the choice is up to you.

OTHER ESSENTIAL TOOLS OF THE TRADE

A waterproof *indelible* marker pen in either a grey or light brown colour.

Test its waterproofness and don't take for granted any claims on the label – things are not always what they appear to be. Read how and why to test your marker pens on page 31.

An A4 sketch pad.	Rubber.	Graph paper.
Tracing paper.	Ruler.	Strip of canvas for practising
Pencils.	Pair of scissors.	the stitches.

A TIP ON BUYING MATERIALS

We do not recommend that you buy all the wools and threads that you need right at the start of your project. We feel it is very necessary to give yourself some choice when working freely, and it is better not to commit yourself to a large quantity of one colour and then realize that perhaps a lighter shade would have been better. Once you have chosen and thought out your design, go out and buy just *one* of *each* of *several* shades of the threads you might need. For instance, if you need a violet colour then buy it in three different shades rather than commit yourself to just one shade there and then in the shop. You can do this with most of the materials that come in hanks or skeins, and we think that the small initial investment in a few extra skeins to allow yourself the choice is a very wise investment. The unused skeins will not be wasted because you will build up a 'bank' of colours which will make your future choices easier, and which are sure to be used up on other projects. There is no need to worry about dye lots – most of the companies have very high standards and in the small areas we are working a change, if any, would be so slight as to be imperceptible. If you have a very large plain background area (and we certainly hope that you won't after using this book) then more care would be needed and you should buy the wool all at once – but make your colour decision wisely first.

STITCHES

All the stitches used in the designs in this book
are fully described and diagrammed in the stitch
library on pages 145–155

Sometimes too much mystique is placed on the mechanical ability to execute the stitches adeptly, to the point where in many cases it has replaced good design as the fundamental entity of embroidery, canvas-work or tapestry. We would prefer you to think of the stitches simply as patterns, only to be arranged by you in combinations to form pleasing designs. Take our word for it – all the stitches used in the designs in this book are simple to learn and easy to work, so do not be put off by the 'experts'. You will be just as expert once you have worked some of the stitches we show you. Learn them simply by following the numbered sequence on the diagrams, which we have made very easy to follow.

Begin by working the stitches out on a piece of practice canvas – use no. 14 mesh for this purpose and either work separate squares for each stitch to keep for reference, or work a sampler of squares of each type of stitch. Don't worry about having to retain all the sequences of every stitch in your head. We still have diagrams on graph paper and samples of all the stitches we use, and while we remember a lot of them from frequent use, we have to refresh the memory too from time to time. So do not feel inhibited about this or any other aspect of 'stitchery'. It is *not* necessary to know all the stitches before starting on a piece of work.

Next, bear in mind that each stitch is a pattern in itself so it is better to limit your use of stitches as well as your colours when working the small area of the average needlepoint cushion (i.e. 15 × 15 in., 37.5 × 37.5 cm). Simplicity by limitation once again is the rule. You will see in the design illustrated on page 66 that it is possible to use only two stitches, and shades of two colours, to achieve a pleasing and delicate design. Some designs make a more complex use of stitchery for their textures, but they use only stitches of a similar type grouped in borders and filled in with areas of a simple stitch for contrast. Once you start to learn these stitches you won't be able to wait to use them in a design of your own.

Always begin and finish off a thread neatly and securely. The methods shown below are suitable for any of the stitches described in the following pages.

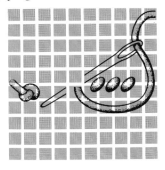 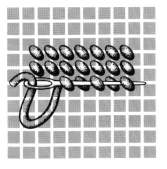

1. Simply pull your needle through at the starting point from back to front of the canvas, leaving a small tail of thread about 2 in. (5 cm) long at the back. Hold this down with your other hand and catch it up under your stitches as you sew.

2. A waste (or temporary) knot. Make a knot at the end of your thread. This knot will be on the front of your canvas and will be cut off later. Insert the needle about 6 or 8 holes away from your proposed starting point and pull through from back to front at the point where you wish to start. Work stitches in the normal way, but catching up the piece of thread at the back. Cut off the knot.

3. If your canvas is already partly worked you can weave your needle under and over three or four stitches and then back again on the wrong side of the work.

Finishing. To finish a thread use the same weaving technique as in (3) above – weave your needle under and over three or four stitches and then back again to secure. Clip off thread neatly.

Try to vary your starting and finishing points so that they don't all come at the same point on your canvas as this would cause a lump made by the slight thickening of the stitches.

TECHNIQUES

Essential information on preparing the canvas,
and methods for finishing and making up.

1. Cutting the canvas

Be sure to *cut your canvas large enough* for your project. We recommend a cushion size of 15 × 15 in. (37.5 × 37.5 cm) as the ideal size for needlepoint. If your design has a definite predetermined size and shape (unlike most of the designs in this book) then you must add a 2 in. (5 cm) margin all round. Your cut piece of canvas would then measure 19 × 19 in. (47.5 × 47.5 cm) (see diagram).

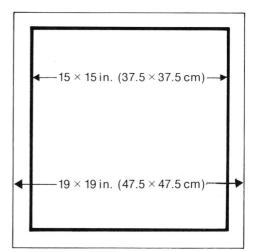

15 × 15 in. (37.5 × 37.5 cm)

19 × 19 in. (47.5 × 47.5 cm)

If you wish to make a smaller or larger cushion, just remember that you must add the extra 2 inches (5 cm) *all round* when cutting the canvas. This extra canvas is needed for blocking and stretching the design and also allows for two rows of tent stitch all round your finished design, necessary when it is made up into a cushion so that a bit of the finished design is not lost under the edges of the fabric backing.

If you are going to work a design that will *grow* from a central point and, like most of the designs in this book, is not predetermined in size and shape, (for instance, if you have only the centre motif or centre panel worked out and then intend to add layers or borders interspersed with areas of background) then this is not the time to be stingy with the canvas. You must allow yourself the freedom of extra canvas for this sort of design growth, so leave an extra 4 or 5 inches (10 or 12 cm) on each side of the basic design size, e.g. a 15 × 15 in. (37.5 × 37.5 cm) design would become a 25 × 25 in. (62 × 62 cm) cut canvas size. Again, this depends on how large you intend your design to be, but if you add the extra 5 inches (12.5 cm) all round you won't regret it later.

N.B. A point to watch out for, and a very common mistake when calculating the size to cut, is to add the extra inches to only one side, e.g. 15 × 15 in. (37.5 × 37.5 cm) plus an extra 2 in. (5 cm) makes 17 × 17 in. (42.5 × 42.5 cm). WRONG! Remember, you are adding *to all sides*, so

2 inches (5 cm) at the top and 2 inches at the bottom is a total of 4 inches (10 cm). The size of the canvas to be cut becomes 19 × 19 in. (47.5 × 47.5 cm).

2. Bind all edges

The reasons for binding the edges of your canvas before working are to keep the canvas from unravelling and also to give you a strong, closely woven surface to which to attach the drawing pins if you need to stretch the finished canvas. See pages 33–36.

We sew a beige folded binding ribbon ($\frac{1}{2}$ inch (1 cm) when folded, one inch (2.5 cm) wide total width) around the edge of the canvases used in our classes because it looks so much more attractive. Masking tape is usually recommended, but make sure that the adhesive on the tape is strong enough to hold it to the canvas. A fabric tape, like a carpet tape, is perfect for binding – we use a tape $1\frac{1}{2}$ in. (3.8 cm) wide.

Alternatively you can oversew the edges of your canvas using a blanket stitch, or run two or three rows of machine zig-zag stitch around the edges.

3. Counting threads

If you are planning a design where you need to count the threads, find the approximate centre of your canvas by folding it into quarters and mark the centre with a cross.

YOUR DESIGN SKETCH

If you intend to improvize patterns and stitches you need only a basic outline of your design on canvas.

More complex designs may require more detailed planning at the design sketch stage. This can be achieved either by tracing or counting.

1. Tracing a design

When you have chosen the design source that you want to use, a piece of tracing paper is the answer. Place this over the piece of wallpaper, fabric, magazine design or whatever it is, and trace off as much detail as you need, (usually only a simple outline). Remember that you can use designs from several sources to build up your design sketch.

27

If the source that you use happens to be the size that you need for your final design, this tracing then becomes your final design outline which you will then transfer on to canvas. If your design sources are either larger or smaller than required you can have your tracing enlarged or reduced at a photocopying shop. (Most up-to-date photocopiers enlarge and reduce, as well as duplicate, and most offices have good ones.) Any shop that specializes in photocopying and duplicating will be able to give you a copy of your tracing, quite inexpensively, that will be the size that you need.

Other methods for enlarging and reducing designs by drawing squares and grids or by using pentographs are complex and unnecessary unless you enjoy the technical process – we don't and we use a photocopier.

One invaluable piece of machinery in our studio that does the job is an *opaque projector*. This overhead projector will allow you to use a photograph or any printed design source that is opaque, (that is, you can't see through it, as opposed to a slide which is transparent and is shown through a normal slide projector) and the machine will enlarge it or reduce it on the surface below. From there the design can be copied on to a piece of paper from the projected image of your design in the size you want. These projectors are splendid, but are a luxury and an unnecessary expense unless you do a lot of design work. Most design studios and art departments have one, however, and it might always be possible to persuade a friend to help you out.

2. Counting a design

If your design requires accuracy and a mathematical approach, such as a dividing up of the design to include specific border areas, mathematically constructed motifs or geometrical patterns, you must be prepared to do a bit of tedious work at this stage. There are no short cuts, each stitch or thread must be counted.

A piece of graph paper is a good start to planning a design of this sort. There are different sizes of graph paper, one of them possibly the same size as the mesh of your canvas. In any case try to find a size as close to your canvas as possible. (But remember that no canvas is perfect and the mesh count may be slightly different vertically or horizontally. That is why your design may vary length and width even if you have counted the same number of threads, or holes, in each direction.) The easiest graph paper to work with is ten squares to the inch, and better still, further divided into squares of 10 × 10, or 100 squares to the square inch.

SHAPES FOR YOUR CUSHIONS
It seems to us that everyone makes square cushions simply because they don't know how to draw other shapes. The basic geometry you learned at school will come in handy now.

1. A square or a rectangle
Draw a straight line, using a ruler, at one side of your design area. Use a right angle set square to draw a perpendicular line. Then measure each side of your square or rectangle, drawing right angles for each corner.

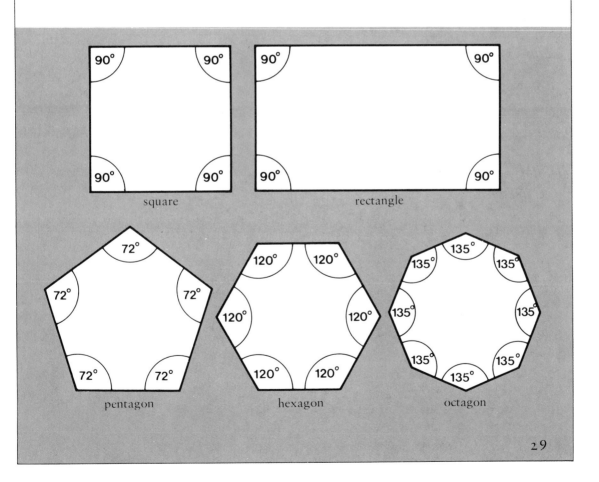

square rectangle

pentagon hexagon octagon

29

2. A circle

Use a pair of compasses to draw a circle. If the radius of your compasses is not large enough to draw a circle the size of your project, draw it approximately half-size and have it enlarged at a photocopier's (see page 28, enlarging a design). If you happen to know an architect or engineer, or a student of draughtsmanship, he or she is likely to be able to help you easily or will lend you the simple equipment. For example, *a beam compass* is used to draw large circles and we use one to do all our circular designs.

All the following shapes have *equal sides* so remember to draw each line the same length.

3. A pentagon

This is a five-sided shape, rather unusual for a needlepoint cushion, which might be just the answer for a project with interesting shapes and border patterns. To draw a pentagon, start with a straight line near the bottom of your paper. Then use a protractor to draw angles of 72° at each end of your line. (You will have to estimate the overall size of your design while drawing your basic pentagon, but you can make it smaller or larger once you have completed it on paper by drawing parallel lines to your first pentagon.) After completing the first two lines draw another angle of 72° at the end of each line and they should meet at a point at the top.

4. A hexagon

This is a six-sided shape that is perfect to accent a sofa. Draw a straight line at the bottom of your paper and draw lines at angles of 60°, and your shape will now have six sides.

5. An octagon

We used this shape for our peony cushion design (page 68) as we needed a more elaborate shape to surround the simple centre motif, and the eight-sided figure was perfect. To draw an octagon start with a straight line at the bottom of your paper. Then draw a line at an angle of 135°, and continue to draw lines of equal length and angles of 135°, until you have an octagon.

Other shapes may evolve free-form and if they look good, refine them. Don't be limited to a square – there are alternatives!

TRANSFERRING YOUR DESIGN TO CANVAS

When your design sketch has enough outline for reference it is ready to be transferred to the canvas. Use as much, or as little, detail as you need to guide you. We usually outline areas of borders and motifs, and in cases where we have decided at this stage where some colour changes are to occur we indicate this on the canvas. The method to use is an easy one.

1. Make sure that the outlines on the design sketch are easy to see, heavy and clear.

2. Place your piece of canvas over your design sketch. Try to align the horizontal and vertical threads of the canvas with the outline shape of your design. You will be able to see the outline of your design sketch quite clearly through the holes in the canvas. As canvas is an uneven woven fabric you may have to move your canvas at times in order to get some of your geometrically arranged lines in their proper position as you transfer them to your canvas.

3. Using a grey or a light tan permanent, waterproof, indelible marker pen trace the outline from the paper on to your canvas. We cannot emphasize enough how important it is thoroughly to test any marker pen *before* you use it on your canvas. Just take a piece of scrap canvas, draw a square about 5 threads × 5 threads and allow it to dry. Now wet it and rub it. If it bleeds into the unmarked part of your canvas then it is unacceptable. Many markers are waterproof or permanent but as dyes both in paints and marker pens may vary from tube to tube or pen to pen, you *must test it yourself.*

USING PAINTS AND MARKER PENS ON CANVAS

We paint on canvas very rarely as most of our designs are composed of textures and stitches and colour, as opposed to the traditional needle-point picture approach which uses just two stitches and relies upon a pre-painted colour design on the canvas to serve as a guide for the wool. But in some designs you may want to do a more detailed guide or outline on your canvas. If you have a centre motif, or a border pattern that you have drawn in colour on your design sketch, and want it exactly like that on your canvas then you need to know more about the techniques of painting on canvas. We used this system exclusively on the Overthorpe Hall tapestry project (see page 136), as the children needed their designs in full colour on the canvas.

Marker pens

We love to use marker pens both on paper and on canvas; they are so easy to use and are accurate if they have a fine point. If you have markers marked *waterproof* or *permanent*, theoretically they should be acceptable, but they must be *tested* before you use them (as described on the previous page). Once any colour is put on to the canvas it must be waterproof, so that when you block or stretch your finished work the colours do not run into your wools and ruin your project. We've found Pentel permanent markers to be generally good, but all pens should be tested before use. You will gradually build up a set of colours that are safe to use on canvas.

Paints

The best effects come from using oil or acrylic paints on the canvas. These require more technique to use than marker pens but if you want more subtle effects than the basic areas of colour definition possible with markers, learn to use acrylics or oils. We use acrylics, as they are water soluble and can easily be thinned. They also wash out easily if they are spilled, dry quickly and are absolutely waterproof once dry on the canvas.

Oil paints are spirit-based and therefore more difficult to use, take longer to dry and are very hard to remove if they are spilled. There are many good brands of acrylics which now come in a great variety of colours. Artists' nylon brushes are perfect for this job as the more expensive sable brushes used for watercolours (never use watercolours on canvas) and oils can be ruined by acrylic paint drying hard on the bristles.

When we have painted the canvas, just to make certain that the paint is waterproof, we brush a light layer of clear acrylic medium over the painted areas. Rowney Cryla is a good one and it gives your marker pen or painted lines a coating of acrylic emulsion, which acts as an extra bit of insurance to make your guide lines permanent.

Don't be afraid to use paints or markers even if you have never done so before. You will learn to use them easily and they are only for your own reference on your canvas, not to create a finished work of art.

ALPHABETS AND NUMBERS

One way to personalize your work is to use initials, monograms or letters to spell out a message. In Anabelle's poem to Fido (see page 127) we used a simple alphabet, as we also did in the Pepsi brick (see page 110).

As canvas is made up of horizontal and vertical threads that create square shapes, it is very difficult to make curves on canvas. Letters and numbers should ideally be square in shape. Curved lettering needs more stitches, which can only be achieved with a larger working area or a smaller mesh canvas.

Fortunately, there are some excellent books devoted entirely to needlepoint and embroidery alphabets. You need only go into your local bookshop or library and ask for charted needlepoint alphabets and you will find a selection. Dover Books publish some good ones, for example, which are sold both in the UK and the US. They include *Needlework Alphabets and Designs*, edited by Blanche Cirker and, more elaborate in style, *Charted Monograms for Needlepoint and Cross Stitch* edited by Rita Weiss. Your local needlework shop will also have some less expensive leaflets produced by wool companies such as J. & P. Coats and DMC. Coats publish a very good booklet called *Alphabets and Numerals* which you may find useful. You should have no difficulty in finding exactly what you want.

Once you have chosen an alphabet style that suits your design and is an appropriate size, it is easy (if rather tedious) to count it out on to the canvas. Take care to be absolutely accurate – there are no short cuts!

BLOCKING OR STRETCHING YOUR WORKED CANVAS

Certain stitches tend to pull diagonally on your canvas more than others (tent stitch distorts the most), and after having worked your project you may be left with a diamond-shaped object which used to be your canvas square. This is perfectly normal; don't worry about it because you can easily stretch it back into its intended shape. One way normally suggested to minimize this distortion is to use a frame to secure the horizontal and vertical threads of your canvas as you work and to resist the pull of the individual stitches. We don't use a frame as we find it inhibiting (we like to roll up our canvas and take it with us) and using a frame demands that you work your needle down through the top surface and up from underneath – two movements – whereas when you hold your canvas in your hands you can get a freer working rhythm.

Blocking is the way to re-shape your canvas after the stitching is complete. This simple process will even out the appearance of your stitches and minimize the differences due to uneven stitch tension. As the materials you used are colourfast (see section on materials, page 15, and techniques, page 25) and the woven effect of needlepoint stitches on canvas creates a very strong, durable fabric, stretching the finished work back into shape is the simple answer.

You do this by wetting your canvas, placing it on a firm piece of board, and pulling it back into the shape you want. Then it is fastened to a piece of board with drawing pins, tacks or staples (through the binding on each side) to keep this shape, and left to dry naturally for 24 to 48 hours. We use a staple gun which is fast, effective, and the staples are easily removed with a screwdriver.

1. The first thing that you need is *a piece of board* to pin the canvas to. It must not warp and it must be soft enough to allow you to put drawing pins in it, yet hard enough to keep these pins secure. Hardboard is too hard and a very soft wood would not be strong enough for repeated use. Pine or plywood is fine. For years we have used one side of a packing crate that is just the right size and is four feet (just over a metre) high, so it serves as a small blocking table.

2. Make sure that the edges of your canvas are properly bound so that the canvas will not unravel during stretching and that the drawing pins will secure the canvas without the edge tearing away or moving. (See binding your canvas, page 27.)

3. Mark the outline of your final design sketch shape on to a piece of brown paper and secure it to your board. (In some designs where you

34

have added rows of stitches or borders you will not have an outline on paper. In these cases measure the length and width of your canvas, add $\frac{1}{4}$ inch ($\frac{1}{2}$ cm) and re-draw an accurate outline. See how to draw shapes, page 29.) This will give you your guidelines for the shape you want your canvas to be.

4. Dampen the canvas with a clean damp cloth or a sponge. Don't submerge it into a sink full of water, but dampen it thoroughly. It will become limp as the sizing that stiffens the canvas dissolves – don't panic!

5. Place your limp canvas, face down, on the paper-covered board and line up the top edge of your worked design with the top line of your paper. Put one tack in each of the four corners to start with.

6. Firmly secure the bound edge of the canvas to the board with drawing pins, thumb tacks, or staples from a staple gun. (Remember that once the canvas is dry you will have to get these out again). Try to use rust-proof pins, such as stainless steel, or be sure to allow enough blank canvas (about $1\frac{1}{2}$ inches or 4 cm) between the pin on the edge and your worked canvas, as rust can run from the metal into the canvas. You may need as many as 10 or 15 pins per side, as it is important to get a straight edge, not a series of peaks.

We begin at the top edge, then do one side, then the other side, with the bottom edge left for last. The last side is the difficult one as it must stretch the tacked canvas to its intended shape and it may offer resistance. Put as many tacks in as are needed to secure the straight line.

7. Let the canvas dry naturally indoors. Don't put it near a radiator or use a hair dryer to speed up the process. It will take 24 to 48 hours and the canvas will be stiff again when it is dry. Remove the tacks or pins gently with a screwdriver, or else you'll take the heads off the tacks and leave the pin part in your board.

If the stretching process hasn't done a good enough job, repeat it – the canvas will take the blocking procedure again. Some books recommend spreading rabbit skin glue or some other 'non-live' glue in a thin film on the wrong side of your canvas after you have stretched it on to the board.

The glue helps to keep the shape secure but it is not necessary nor recommended except in extreme cases where normal blocking, without glue, doesn't work.

MAKING UP A CUSHION

Types of cushions

There are two types of cushions; the knife-edge where the sides are seamed together, and the box-edge where a gusset is inset between the canvas and the back of the cushion to form a box shape.

The knife-edge type, filled with its feather inner cushion, gives a more rounded surface and you therefore tend to lose sight of the edges of your design. But if you prefer the appearance of this type of cushion, then you can compensate for the visual loss of your borders by adding extra rows of tent stitches around the edges. Or you may not feel that this is necessary if the centre is the most important visual part of your design.

The box-edge cushion gives a flat surface so that all the design is visible. This is important where the borders form a strong part of the design.

Some of our own designs (see pages 61–118) definitely needed box-edges – for example the lime green Spanish rug cushion and the octagonal peony design, but others like the blue and cream lace design needed the softer appearance of the knife-edge, even though the border is important. So your design should dictate your choice.

Edgings

All cushions look better finished off with an edging of piping or cord. You could make up a cord using the wools in the colours of your design and you could add tassels too if you think it would compliment the design. Instructions on how to make cords and tassels are given opposite and page 38.

Finishing services

You can have your canvas stretched and blocked and made up into a cushion by a professional finishing service. Of course, this will be rather expensive but you will have a beautifully made cushion and we recommend it for those of you who are not very good with the sewing needle or machine. It would be a pity to put all your creative efforts into your design only to mar it with the finishing touches. Of course, those of you who are good seamstresses will be able to do it yourselves.

A TIP ON BUYING FABRICS FOR FINISHING CUSHIONS

For some reason the fabric most often chosen to back needlepoint cushions is velvet – but this seems to us to give a very dull appearance. Much more attractive, we think, is a fabric with a lustre. This contrasts beautifully with a cushion worked mainly in wool, giving it a lighter quality, and lends an added glow to a cushion containing some shine. There are many attractive fabrics in the stores. You will notice that all the cushions in this book are backed with a lovely moiré silk, mainly because it is a favourite fabric of ours, but also because it comes in a lovely range of colours from the soft and muted to the deep and glowing. Its crisp texture adds firmness to the finished cushion, too. The price of this type of fabric ranges from medium to expensive but the colour ranges are excellent at both levels.

With a theme like Anabelle's Ice-Cream cushion, then a crisp heavy furnishing cotton picking up similar colours is very jolly and in keeping with the fun of the article.

If you are using a finishing service, it is best to ask exactly how much fabric will be required as this seems to vary from place to place. Check carefully too if you use a fabric with a pattern which has to be used from top to bottom. If you are making up the cushion yourself then do make sure you buy enough to do it properly. A metre should allow you enough for box-edges and piping.

HOW TO MAKE A WOOLLEN CORD EDGING

Many of your projects will be enhanced by the addition of some form of decorative trim. Cushions worked mainly in wool look good edged with a matching, twisted wool cord. Choose wool in the shade that best complements your finished project and cut several strands of it three times the length required for the edge or area you intend to cover. Twist the strands tightly together until they begin to kink, then fold them in half and twist them again to make a woollen cord. The number of strands that you use depends upon the intended thickness of your finished cord after you have twisted, and then doubled your wool.

HOW TO MAKE TASSELS

Tassels can be a very effective decorative extra for a cushion and they are surprisingly simple to make. Take a piece of cardboard about 3 in. square (7.5 cm) and wind your wool or other thread around the card approximately thirty times. Once again how many times depends on the thickness of the wool and the eventual plumpness of the tassel that you want. Tie the strands together at one end of the card to secure the top of the tassel, and cut through the strands at the other end of the card. Tie these doubled strands about one inch from the top with a separate piece of wool.

JOINING TOGETHER A LARGE TAPESTRY PROJECT

In the case of a group project worked by a number of different individuals (for example the Overthorpe Hall tapestry, page 135) all the separate components finally have to be joined together to make a complete tapestry. There are several important factors to be borne in mind.

It is only possible to join pieces of the same-sized canvas together, and because in canvas of the same mesh size the horizontal mesh count is different from the vertical mesh, you must match the canvases to be joined either horizontal to horizontal or vertical to vertical. This needs careful pre-planning when the project is laid out and the sections distributed. We did this in the Overthorpe Hall tapestry and we indicated, on each piece of cut canvas, which was the top. Every design was planned and worked in the same direction so that each one could be joined up properly when complete.

Even with careful pre-planning it is very difficult to get each section joined perfectly, as stitch tension varies from person to person and even within one's own work, so no worked piece of canvas is exactly the same finished size as another. Bearing this in mind, there are two methods that we would recommend for joining canvases together.

Simple seam method

Once you have worked your canvases and blocked them, sew them together with a flat seam by backstitching through the last row of worked stitches. Be sure to match your backstitches, mesh for mesh (hole for hole) with your needlepoint stitch. Then you need only fold the excess canvas back, mitre the corners and blind stitch the excess to the back of the needlepoint stitches. If there is too much canvas ($\frac{1}{2}$ in. or 1 cm is sufficient) trim away the excess, including your edge binding.

Cut edge over cut edge method

Leave at least four unworked rows of canvas holes all round each piece of canvas to be joined. Place one piece over the other, overlapping three rows of holes and making sure that the holes match exactly. Pin the two pieces of canvas together, then baste stitch them together down the centre holes of the overlapped canvas to join them temporarily. If you are joining mono (single) mesh canvas, as opposed either to double mesh or to interlock canvas, you may have to put a thin line of quick-set glue across the top edge of the cut canvas to keep the threads of the canvas from unravelling (we use UHU).

Working from the edge of one of the finished canvases and using the same stitch as used for the last rows of your worked canvas (this would normally be tent stitch), stitch the canvas row by row, through the overlapped pieces until these rows are completed. You may have to use an 'up and down' motion inserting your needle as you would if you were using a frame. This will prevent the overlapping meshes from falling out of line as they are pulled by the stitch.

PREPARING A CANVAS FOR FRAMING

Some designs are ideally suited for display on the wall, in particular childrens' designs which are really woven pictures. We've found that the best way to prepare these designs is to stretch them over a piece of firm board and secure the canvas with drawing pins on the back. Once the canvas is stretched and mounted on a piece of board you can add a frame (without glass) to create a more finished appearance.

Framing and mounting hints

1. Work four extra rows of tent stitch all round your finished work.

2. Cut plywood or hardwood $\frac{1}{8}$ inch ($\frac{1}{4}$ cm) smaller all round than your design (including the four extra rows). This will ensure that the wrapped-around edge will not expose any unworked canvas.

3. For a softer, padded look cotton batting can be used to cover the board before the worked canvas is stretched over it.

4. Stretch the worked canvas tightly over the board and secure the edges on the back side of the board with drawing pins.

5. When securely pinned, cut away any excess canvas, especially in the corners. Mitre the corners if you like and whipstitch the folds in each corner.

We feel that most needlepoint pictures look pretty enough to be hung on the wall without adding a frame. However, if you prefer the 'finished' look of a frame, all you need to do is enclose this mounted canvas in a suitable frame. If you do intend to frame the board, remember that the edge of a frame will cover a small edge of your worked canvas (anywhere from $\frac{1}{8}$ of an inch to more than $\frac{1}{4}$ of an inch or $\frac{1}{4}$ to $\frac{1}{2}$ a centimetre, depending upon the size of the frame that you choose). So you need to add sufficient rows of tent stitch around the outside edges of your finished design to allow the frame to cover your extra stitches and not part of your design.

PHOTOGRAPH FRAMES

A photograph frame in needlepoint is a pretty, accessible project and we show two examples on the same theme in the section on designs, page 100.

The technique for mounting the worked canvas on a wooden frame is exactly the same as described above, except of course that extra rows of tent stitch should be worked around both the inner and the outer edges. We do suggest that you pad the wooden frame first with cotton batting to give a softer, more rounded effect. Canvas over bare wood can sometimes look thin and strained.

Finish off the frame with a thin board backing to enclose the photograph and to which a little stand can be fixed.

THE FIRST DESIGN
LETTERS

This is a marvellous – and very simple – first
exercise for beginners, as it offers an opportunity
to use the three different and necessary elements
of needlepoint design.

These three elements are:

(a) Practice in working different stitches and combining them in a design form, rather than simply working small squares as a sampler. This exercise helps you to learn how to fit the stitches into various odd shapes which you will have to do when working your own design.

(b) The opportunity to use several different threads so that you discover their separate qualities and how they look when used in different stitches.

(c) Practice in the use of light, medium and dark tones – made easier by using *only one* colour. We suggest you use one colour of wool in three tones – light, medium and dark, plus a stranded cotton, a perlé cotton and a soft embroidery cotton in the same colour but each one in a different tone value. For example, the wool might be in a light, a medium and a dark green, the stranded cotton in light green, the perlé cotton in a medium/light green and the soft embroidery cotton in a medium/dark green. This will help you to see how the tones work in the different threads; for example the shiny stranded cotton and perlé give a much lighter appearance than, for instance, the matte soft embroidery cotton, or the wool, because of their reflective quality. (See sections on colour [page 53 and ff.] and materials [page 15 and ff.] for a fuller explanation.)

ADLER COLOUR PACKS

Knowing how difficult and frustrating it can be trying to obtain all the materials you need locally, we have put together six different Colour Packs based on this one-colour theme and all in the pastel colours that we use in our designs. The packs contain all the different types of threads to do the lettering exercise described here, or could also be the basis of any other design of your own. You can, of course, add more colours as you progress, but this one-colour approach will give you a good start in using the methods we describe in more detail in the following chapters. As well as the different threads the packs include a square of no. 14 single mesh canvas bound with a soft woven ribbon – if you are going to work something beautiful even your canvas should look and feel good – and which has our Adler label.

> In detail, each Adler Colour Pack contains:
>   square of first quality canvas, no. 14 single mesh
>   size 15 × 15 inches (38 × 38cm), bound with ribbon.
> $\frac{1}{2}$ oz of strandable wool in a light tone
> $\frac{1}{2}$ oz of strandable wool in a medium tone
> $\frac{1}{2}$ oz of strandable wool in a dark tone
>   2 skeins of perlé cotton
>   2 skeins of stranded cotton
>   1 skein of soft embroidery cotton
>   1 pack of no. 18 tapestry needles
> The seven different colour choices are in delicate tones of:
>   peach/apricot;   delicate greens;   soft blues;
>   soft true pinks;   delicate yellows;
>   bronze/apricot;   soft cream/beige.
> To order the Colour Packs, see page 143.

Obviously it is impossible to estimate exactly how much of each thread you will need to complete your design – that depends on the design and how you use the threads, so if you find that you need more of a certain colour of any of the threads, they can be reordered by mail.

MAKING YOUR OWN DESIGNS

You will need: Sketch paper   Glue
   A magazine   Pencil   Square of canvas size 15 × 15
   Paper scissors   Indelible marker pen   inches (38 × 38cm).

How to do it
1. Begin by looking through the magazine and noticing the different types of lettering. Do not be inhibited by the fact that these are letters and

initials – they are not necessarily going to be used as such. Think of them as graphic shapes with a recognizable form. Choose large letters, bold enough to fill space, and cut out your initials, or just one letter if you prefer.

2. Draw a 10 × 10 in. (25 × 25 cm) square on a piece of sketch paper.

3. Place the cut out letters on the sketch paper within the square and move them around until a pleasing arrangement appears. If you want to make one letter more dominant, overlay it on the other. You should be observing the breakdown of the shapes that appear with the different arrangements. When your letters are arranged satisfactorily stick them in place on the sketch paper.

4. With a marker pen draw outlines around the letters.

5. Draw a 10 × 10 in. (25 × 25 cm) square on your canvas using an indelible marker pen. (Test the pen *first* before marking the canvas. See page 31 for how to do this.)

6. Place the canvas over the letters, lining up the two squares.

7. The outlines of the letters will be visible through the holes in the canvas. Trace them onto your canvas using an indelible marker pen.

The illustrated example used the letters R A and we placed them in a very simple overlapping arrangement. Remember we were using the letters to break down areas and not as a monogram, and where the letters overlapped at the bottom a triangle was formed. As there was already a triangle in the centre of the A this gave us the idea of breaking the areas down into further triangles where the lines followed logically.

In this case the design was worked from the large vertical area of the R. This section was worked first and a sequence of stitches, colours and threads established and the design was then worked outwards from this point. If you adopt the same method of working you will be able to place each stitch, colour tone and texture of thread in sequence. This is vital in all needlepoint designs. If you work small areas over the canvas and then try to unite them the design will be spotty and you may not get a happy combination of colour tones and textures.

If we explain this design in detail in working sequence you will see how, starting with the basic areas that appeared on the paper, we broke these down into further areas of pattern as the design was stitched.

Analysis:

CANVAS No. 14 single mesh. Design size approximately $9\frac{1}{2} \times 6\frac{1}{2}$ in. (24×16.5 cm).

COLOURS All in the apricot through to bronze colour family, used in different tone values.

Wool: medium apricot No 4: pale apricot No 1
Stranded cotton: light apricot Anchor 0336
Soft embroidery cotton: dark bronze DMC 2632
Perlé: medium/dark bronze DMC 407

TEXTURES Strandable wool split to one strand, stranded cotton used unsplit, soft embroidery cotton and perlé cotton.

STITCHES Tent, cross, Scottish, Scottish with tent and double leviathan.

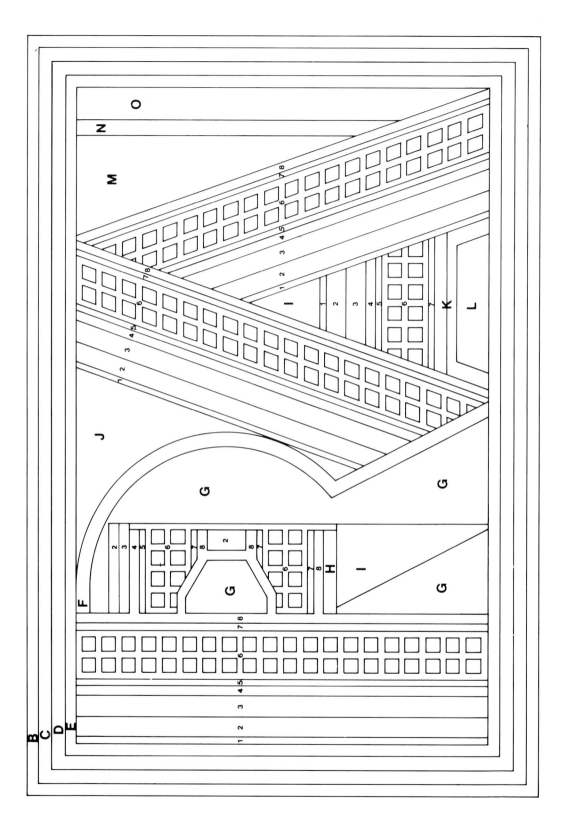

B   tent light apricot SC

C   double leviathan medium/dark bronze perlé

D   double leviathan light apricot SC

E   three rows tent medium apricot wool

F   two rows cross dark bronze SEC

G   cross medium/dark bronze perlé

H   Scottish medium/dark bronze perlé

I   tent dark bronze SEC

J   cross light apricot SC

K   two rows cross dark bronze SEC

L   three rows cross medium/dark bronze perlé

M   five rows cross light apricot SC

N   two rows cross dark bronze SEC

O   four rows cross medium/dark bronze perlé

1   tent medium/dark bronze perlé

2   double leviathan medium/dark bronze perlé

3   double leviathan pale apricot wool

4   cross medium apricot wool

5   tent light apricot SC

6   Scottish/tent outlines with medium/dark bronze perlé, filled in with pale apricot wool

7   tent light apricot SC

8   cross medium apricot wool

SC = stranded cotton
SEC = soft embroidery cotton

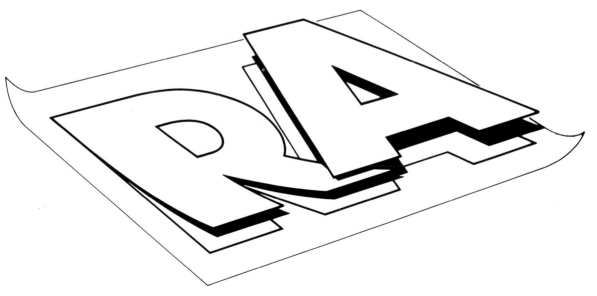

Construction

We started with the vertical line of the R and established a bold sequence of stitches using all the threads with the exception of the soft embroidery thread in the darkest colour, and using two different large 'square' stitches, the double leviathan and Scottish stitch with tent, to form a band of pattern. (This band of pattern was later used throughout the design, worked horizontally on the inner section of the R and on the crossband of the A, and tilted on the diagonal lines of the A. This is indicated on the diagram in sequence by the numbers 1 through 8 and the sequence of stitches listed at the side.) The curve of the R was outlined next in the dark bronze soft embroidery cotton. With the establishment of these areas interesting triangular shapes emerged at the bottom of the R and these were filled in with medium bronze perlé cross stitches and dark bronze soft embroidery cotton in tent stitch. The curves of the R were filled in to match the perlé medium bronze triangle at the bottom. The pattern sequence was then worked horizontally to fill in the remaining area.

The next area worked was the left slope of the A using the pattern sequence. This was repeated on the right hand slope and also in the crossband.

The inner triangle of the A was stitched in tent stitch using the dark bronze soft embroidery cotton to balance the similar triangle at bottom left. The area beneath the A crossband was worked in a stripe of cross stitches using dark bronze soft embroidery cotton and medium bronze perlé and this stripe was repeated down the right hand side of the canvas.

The background was filled in using light apricot stranded cotton in cross stitch (filled in with tent stitch where there was not enough room to make complete crosses).

Three rows of tent stitch in medium apricot wool were worked around the design area to make a division between the design and the border.

Two rows of double leviathan stitches (1) in light apricot stranded cotton and (2) in medium bronze perlé form the border and a row of tent stitches in light apricot stranded cotton gave this a neat finishing edge. A further three rows of tent stitch were worked for making up purposes.

Working comments

Establishing a pattern sequence of stitches, textures and colours to be repeated throughout the design gives the piece a visual continuity. This technique of repeating areas of pattern in a design that is basically not symmetrical can also add balance to the design. You will notice that a small second stripe of pattern (the cross stitches in medium bronze and dark bronze used under the A) is also repeated down the right hand side, giving a pleasing balance to the area. The same technique is used to balance areas of similar shape – for instance, the repeating triangles on each side, using the same thread and stitch. By breaking down the design into further shapes as we went along, repeat areas were found – for example, the triangles at the bottom left hand side repeating the centre triangle of the A.

You will notice how the texture of the stitch used can slightly change the tone value of the thread – for example, the stronger contrast of the soft embroidery thread in dark bronze worked in tent stitch with the medium bronze perlé worked in cross stitch in the bottom left hand corner, compared with the slightly lesser contrast of these two colours and threads when using the same cross stitch.

Although we originally started out with three wools in the dark, medium and light tones we found that we didn't need to use all three in this design, and you may find that you will not use one or other of your chosen threads because with the establishment of your pattern it may become too much.

In some places, for example the crossband of the A, our strip of pattern was larger than the marked area on the canvas, and we simply enlarged this area when working it to suit our pattern, making the inner triangle smaller. Use your marked outlines as guidelines only. Don't be afraid to adapt your stitches to fit into corners, or simply fill in with tent stitch where there is no room to make a complete larger stitch. For example, our cross stitch background becomes tent stitch in smaller corners.

Making up

When the stitching was finished the work was blocked (see page 33 for how to do this). Working something in a small size can present a problem when it comes to deciding how to make it up. This design was obviously too small for a wall, so we decided that the best approach was to insert the panel in the centre of a larger cushion. If you adopt this plan, however, you must 'frame' the design with an edging. Piping is always useful, but in this case the shiny, textured effect of the double leviathan stitch border, glowing in perlé and stranded cotton, reminded us of furnishing braid. So, to finish off the panel, we enclosed it in a frame of bronze braid and then mounted the whole on a cushion covered in rippling paler bronze moiré silk. The braid frames the design more effectively whilst creating the necessary division between the fabric and design. You could, of course, expand on this theme and add a further row, or rows of the decorative braid close to the edges of the cushion.

50

Above: the Letters Design

Right: the Green Initialled Cushion

COLOUR

Actually, you work with few colours. But they seem like a lot more when each one is in the right place . . .
PICASSO IN *PICASSO ON ART*

The sumptuousness of colour is what first attracted us to needlepoint. When colour combines with the tactile softness of the wools and the glow of threads, it is irresistible.

Just walking into a shop one day and seeing a wall full of wool in colours of glowing softness is what started our needlepoint compulsion. Those of you who have seen this sort of display, especially in the USA, will know the feeling. You just can't wait to use all those shades.

Be warned, though. *The first temptation, and the first mistake, is to choose too many different colours.* In fact for a beginner, that dazzling wall of wool can make choice very difficult without guidance. We will therefore give you some rules and limitations which will make it easier for you to go into a store and choose exactly what you need with confidence. This independence really is necessary as sales-people are not always able to advise – a lot of them simply 'work there', and can only take your money and hand over the goods. (Of course, this is not true of all shops. Some are owned and staffed by enthusiasts who will do everything possible to help you make the right choice.)

In needlepoint, as always in good design, simplicity is best. Too much colour in the relatively small area of a needlepoint canvas creates visual confusion. There are some simple facts to learn about tone values of colours. We divide each colour into **three tones** – light, medium and dark. For example, blue divides into (1) light blue (2) medium blue (3) dark blue.

We then make a further subdivision into (4) pale blue (5) light medium blue (6) medium dark blue. Some of the wools you can buy will be available in this range of tones and would shade like this (see Diagram A):

1. pale blue   3. light/medium blue   5. medium/dark blue
2. light blue   4. medium blue   6. dark blue

These are the colour categories used in the designs in this book. Once you break a colour down into these categories you will soon learn exactly what tone to look for when you are choosing your shades for your work, and the process quickly becomes a habit.

The next step is learning how to use the tones together.

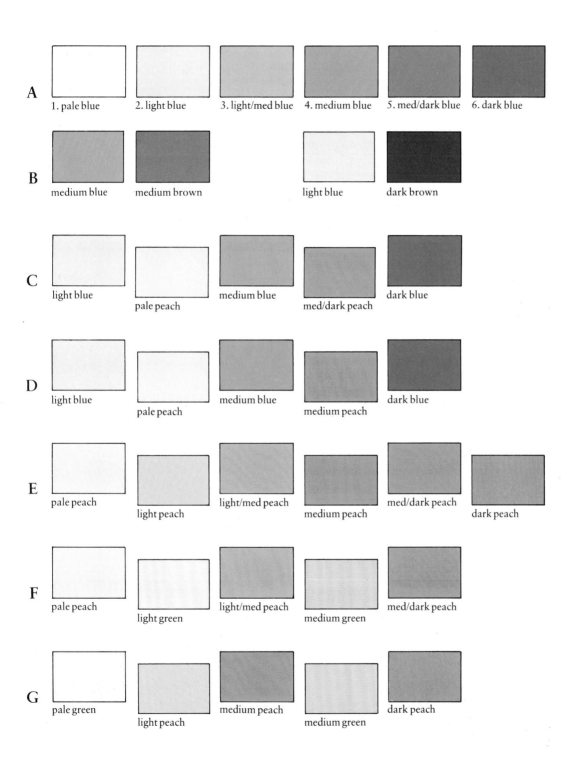

A
1. pale blue   2. light blue   3. light/med blue   4. medium blue   5. med/dark blue   6. dark blue

B
medium blue   medium brown   light blue   dark brown

C
light blue   pale peach   medium blue   med/dark peach   dark blue

D
light blue   pale peach   medium blue   medium peach   dark blue

E
pale peach   light peach   light/med peach   medium peach   med/dark peach   dark peach

F
pale peach   light green   light/med peach   medium green   med/dark peach

G
pale green   light peach   medium peach   medium green   dark peach

Basic colour rule: *never use two colours of the same tone value next to each other.* For example, medium blue and medium brown will simply neutralize each other visually. In other words – no impact!

But if you use a light shade next to a dark shade you will get a more dramatic effect *because* of the strong contrast, e.g. light blue and dark brown (see Diagram B).

If you use a light tone with a medium tone, or a medium tone with a dark tone, there will be less contrast and you will achieve a more subtle, or softer effect.

The way we teach our students the use of colour is by starting them off on the letters design exercise described in Chapter 4. Only one colour is used, but in different tone values, e.g. tones of blue. By giving our students only one colour to work with, we teach them the instinctive use of tones of that colour to obtain the right contrasts. We recommend this method to all beginners for use on their first project because it eliminates the need for picking out a number of colours where a lot of possibly expensive mistakes can be made, and because it gives a good working knowledge of how to use the tones in all future work. This basic colour concept goes hand in hand with the use of the different wools and threads as described in the discussion of textures.

As a footnote to the rules on colour, one thing is worth remembering. When you are working out a colour theme in different types of thread, there is an exception to the rules. The only time that the same tone values can be used next to each other (e.g. two dark colours) is when they are in highly contrasting threads (e.g. dark blue wool and dark blue perlé). The wool has a matte surface which absorbs the light and the perlé has a shiny surface which reflects the light, providing the necessary subtle contrast.

The different textures of thread (as described on pages 16 and 17) provide plenty of variety within the one-colour theme. Try using a light, a medium and a dark wool with a light stranded cotton and a medium tone perlé, for example. Beginners should use the different textures too. In our Adler Colour Packs (see page 42) we use a light, a medium and a dark strandable wool, and a variety of tones in stranded cotton, perlé and soft embroidery cotton.

Once the one-colour theme has been mastered, the next step is to introduce *one* contrasting colour – but again, in two or three tone values, e.g. light, medium and dark blue plus pale peach and medium/dark peach (see Diagrams C and D). If you like, include these in more than one texture of thread, for instance, stranded cotton and wool. You will find that infinite combinations and contrasts are possible within this still-limited colour scheme.

You may feel the urge to use two or three more colours in your second project but we do advise you to try this two-colour approach first. You can see an example of it illustrated on page 66 (the flower cushion) and it demonstrates just how successful this can be, even using only one texture (in this case wool). After this you should be experienced enough to interpret your personal feeling about colour in your work, adding it where you need it but always remembering to limit the number of colours used.

Colour has an emotional appeal to the senses and is a very personal matter. One person's colour choice will not be another's – fortunately. We all have our favourite colour and it crops up again and again in our day-to-day choices, which we have been making for most of our lives, whether they relate to clothes, fabrics, lampshades, carpets – or even food. In fact, the subconscious effect of colour on our senses can play a large part in our choice of food. As a child one of us couldn't eat 'white food' no matter how good it might have smelled and tasted – it simply didn't have any appeal, and still doesn't. (We also know someone who won't eat 'red' food – we'd make a difficult pair of dinner guests!)

So all the designs you see in this book reflect our personal colour preferences. They are offered, as are the designs, as a guide to what can be done rather than as patterns to be copied. If our designs appeal to you, then adapt them for your own – use them as your 'source'. You will see that we love to use the pastel, almost 'chalky', shades of soft colours, and that we rarely use a very hard contrast. To achieve this effect remember the basic rule of always having a light, a medium and a dark shade, but keep them within a *pastel colour palette*.

For example, when using a peach colour we might choose:
(1) pale peach, light/medium peach and medium/dark peach
or
(2) light peach, medium peach and dark peach (see Diagram E).

57

Overleaf: the Iced Blue and Pink Moiré Silk Cushions

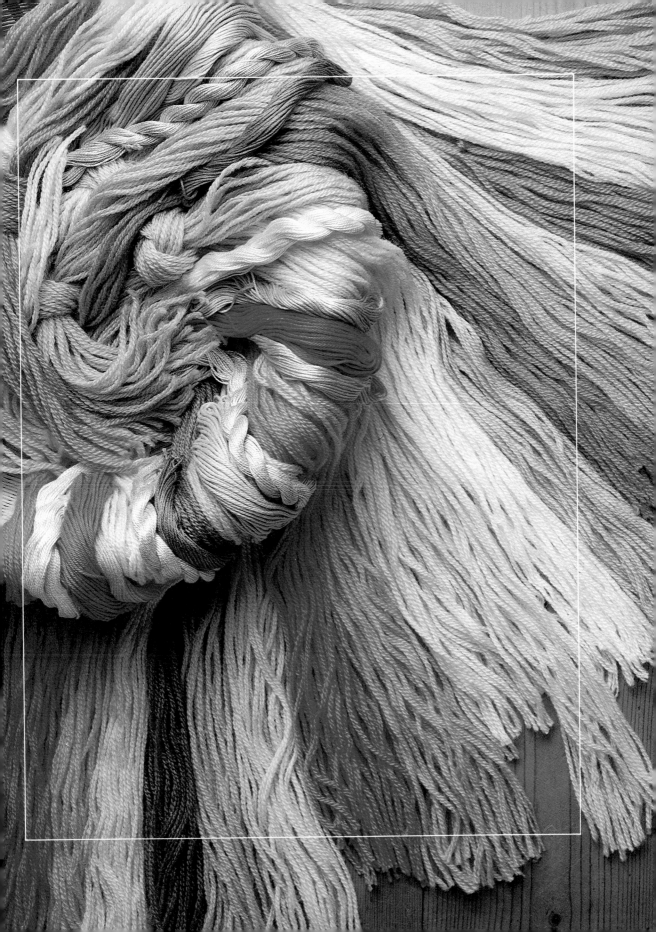

If we add more colours we keep them within the same pastel palette, perhaps adding to group (1) as follows:

pale peach, light green, light/medium peach,
medium green, medium/dark peach (see Diagram F).

This provides enough contrasting tone values without incorporating any dark shades which would make the design too heavy. In group (2) we would add:

pale green, light peach, medium green, medium peach, dark peach (see Diagram G).

We would *not* use the medium green and the medium peach colours next to each other unless we were using a contrasting thread texture.

When choosing a colour scheme we always look for the palest tone of the colours and work from there towards the darkest in tone value. If we wanted a *darker* colour scheme we would do the opposite and choose our darkest colour *first*.

It is not necessary to limit yourself only to light, medium and dark — combine the tone values in any way that pleases you. As long as they are used according to the basic rules the end result will be very effective.

A word about the use of white and black. These are the two strongest contrasts of all, and they are the ones that should be used most sparingly. Pure white is very dominating in a small canvas and you will always be able to find something else that offers the contrast you need, but with a hint of colour. Try magnolia, very soft cream or palest cream beige instead and you will usually discover that there is sufficient contrast and a much prettier effect. Use white only as an accent or where there is an absolute need for such a strong contrast. The same rule applies to black. It is far better to try the deepest shade of blue/black which will give the desired contrast and much more depth but without the dead look of true black, and without such a hard edge.

Take care, too, when using reds with greens. They tend to cancel each other out visually, and it's not a colour combination that we would recommend.

Study the illustrations in this book and they will guide you in your first approaches to using colour in your needlepoint.

THE DESIGNS

Twelve original ideas for needlepoint

In our experience every needlepointer – whether he or she is coming new to needlepoint, or has been doing it for some time – wants to make something for the home. So the theme of this book is how to adapt the decorative themes of your own home surroundings for your needlepoint designs. It is much more interesting and exciting to take design elements and combine them in your own way and to add your personal and individual needlepoint of view than it is to copy a pattern.

The designs illustrated show you how we used our furnishings as a stimulus for shapes, textures and colours and we hope they will point the way for you to do the same. They are meant to guide you to do your own designs, using your home and garden – and even your family – to produce unique decorations for your rooms. If you feel that you can't manage this, and would prefer to copy the designs shown here, then do it – all the information you need is provided. But we would much prefer you to plunge right in and do your own using the elements of design from these illustrations and incorporate them into your own theme.

To help you see more clearly what we have done, we have created a new way of diagramming the designs which makes it easy for you to see the plans and layout of the designs, rather than using the usual complex and eye-wearying charts. This system of line-drawings, listing each row or area with its stitch, colour and thread, will take you easily step by step through the design. In the diagrams we itemize each stitch, thread and colour used (but not the brand name and colour number of the threads as this information is provided in the accompanying text so that you may buy the exact colours used if you wish). A colour might appear in a diagram for example as 'raspberry pink perlé', and would be listed for purchasing purposes in the text as 'raspberry pink perlé DMC 899'.

All the stitches used are described and illustrated in the stitches chapter, page 145 and ff. So if you wish to work the whole piece, or simply to extract a certain sequence of stitches or colours, the diagrams make it simple for you.

The text accompanying each design begins with a paragraph to introduce you to the source of the design and our approach to using it as a theme for needlepoint. The analysis section gives a complete breakdown of the materials, colours and stitches used; the construction paragraph tells exactly how the design was 'constructed'; and the working

62

Three designs taken from the patterned chintz Bakers' Peony Garden design on the sofa. The two cushions on the sofa are the Peony and the Bamboo Designs, while the cushion on the floor is the Small Flower Design

comments give further pointers as to how the design evolved further during the working stages, why certain colours were used and why certain stitches and textures were used in various areas.

So here are the 'ideas'. We hope you will find them attractive and unusual enough to give you the extra little 'push' you might need into designing for needlepoint yourself.

The first three cushions were inspired by a patterned chintz fabric, Bakers' Peony Garden design. The fabric is the upholstery on the sofa in our studio, but it might also be used as curtains or loose covers.

The pattern is a large one with bold motifs, and we have chosen three different ways to use it as a design source for cushions that complement the fabric without simply copying the pattern. The idea is to reflect and enhance the fabric without merely repeating it in stitchery, and the way to do this is to take the pattern as the source and extract one or two elements from it.

In our case, as we were making the cushions to be placed on the sofa, we felt that it was more effective to use the less strong elements in the fabric pattern whilst maintaining the colour theme. For this reason we chose not to use the bird, which already appears on the front of every cushion. However, if we *had* been longing to use the bird in the design we could perhaps have used only part of him – the head for instance.

Another point to consider when making several cushions for a sofa or specific area is to try to vary their sizes and shapes to give a more interesting display.

THE SMALL FLOWER CUSHION

The first method is the simplest. It uses shades of the two main fabric colours, two stitches and only one texture of thread.

64

Analysis

CANVAS No. 16 single mesh. Design size approximately $10\frac{1}{2} \times 10$ in. (27.5 × 25.5 cm).

TEXTURES Strandable wool, used split to 2-ply.

COLOURS *Wool:* pale iced green No 1: light/medium apple green No 3: medium country green No 4: light bronzed coral No 2: light/medium bronzed coral No 3

STITCHES Brick stitch and upright cross stitch (see stitches, page 145 and ff.)
For design diagram, see page 156.

Construction

The pattern and the background are worked entirely in brick stitch. The small border is simply two rows of brick stitch in light/medium green and two in medium green, plus two rows of upright cross stitch in light coral and two in medium coral. The flower motif used as a repeating pattern is based on Bargello (or Florentine) patterns.

Working comments

A delicate repeating pattern like this looks beautiful in soft colours. The very pale green we used as the background colour needed the muted shades of green and coral in the motifs to keep its fresh and delicate feeling. Enough contrast is achieved by keeping the light, medium and dark tone values within a very pale colour range; strong or very dark colour contrasts are not necessary. Although we used the same colour *range* as the fabric, the wool colours are not an exact match. For instance the background colour is paler so that it doesn't blend into the sofa.

This cushion also shows how even a simple border, picking up the colours of the pattern and using one stitch, can set off the design and is as important an element of it as the centre motif or pattern. By taking the colours of the centre motif out into the border we achieved a pleasing balance. The width and shape of the border is dictated by the size and weight of the centre motif or pattern.

The Small Flower Cushion

The Peony Cushion

THE PEONY CUSHION

In the second example we took the main flower design from the fabric – the peony – choosing the white peony with different greens as the colour theme.

Analysis

CANVAS   No. 16 single mesh. Design size approximately 15×14 in. (38×36.5 cm).

TEXTURES   Strandable wool split to 2-ply and stranded cotton, used as a whole strand and not split.

COLOURS   *Wool:* light apple green No 2: medium apple green No 4: light coral No 2: light/medium paprika No 3: soft white No 1 *Stranded cotton:* light silver green Anchor 0842: light/medium apple green Anchor 0843: medium/dark forest green Anchor 0262: medium coral Anchor 08: white Anchor 0402

STITCHES   Tent, cross, upright cross, leaf and brick (see stitches, page 145 and ff.).
For design diagram, see page 157.

Construction

The background was worked in light apple green wool, using brick stitch worked horizontally. The octagonal border was outlined in paprika and worked in alternate panels of upright cross stitch and leaf stitch. The flower petals were worked in a combination of cross stitch and tent stitch using wool and stranded cotton. The flower centre also used tent and cross stitches in stranded cotton. The whole flower was outlined in tent stitch in the green stranded cottons.

Working comments

This cushion used slightly stronger colours than our first design. The background here is an apple green but it is still gentle in colour and blends equally well with the main fabric colours, though again it is not an exact match. Once again we think you can see that it is not necessary to use very strong colour contrasts in order to obtain a dramatic effect. The drama here is achieved by the use of shiny and matte threads (stranded cotton and wool) combined with flat stitches (tent and brick) and raised stitches (cross and upright cross) which give a textural three-dimensional quality even where only one colour is used, as in the white petals.

You can also see how it is possible to use colours of the same tone value next to each other where there is the contrast of a matte thread with a shiny thread, as in the border. This should *never* be done when using threads of the same texture, e.g. two wools, and the same tone value. The only exception would be if you wished to obtain a colour wash effect by using several pastel shades in rows together. Pale blue and pale green, for instance, would give a hazy colour quality for a background.

We traced the flower outline direct from the fabric in pencil, and put it onto the canvas using an indelible marker pen. (This process is described fully in the techniques chapter on page 31.) Only the simplest outline is necessary as a guide. We added a broad octagonal border to balance the heavy asymmetrical flower and to add interest, outlining it in the paprika, echoing the coral from the centre of the flower. (How to mark out an octagonal border is also described fully in the techniques chapter on page 30.)

Above: the Bamboo Cushion

Right: Anabelle's Rose Pink Cushion

THE BAMBOO CUSHION

For the third example we used the bamboo border pattern from the fabric, but as a centre panel rather than as a border. This design is the most complex of the three in its use of stitches, colours and textures. We chose the very palest of the coral shades as the main background colour, and whilst the overall use of the colour was still quite limited, we also picked up the very pale blue used in the small background flower in the fabric and worked this in two textures of thread (wool and stranded cotton) as well as the greens and coral colours. The triangles and rectangles of the bamboo design lend themselves to a geometric pattern and this time we used a variety of stitches in geometric arrangements, in three types of thread.

Analysis

CANVAS   No. 16 single mesh. Design size approximately $15\frac{1}{2} \times 15\frac{1}{2}$ in. (38.5 × 38.5 cm).

TEXTURES   Strandable wool, stranded cotton and perlé.

COLOURS   *Wool:* light fiord green No 2: pale coral No 1: light coral No 2: medium coral No 4: medium/dark coral No 5: light turquoise blue No 2
Stranded cotton: medium green Anchor 0858: pale coral Anchor 06: light silver blue Anchor 0158
Perlé: medium/dark green DMC 320: medium coral DMC 353

STITCHES   Tent, brick, cross, double cross, upright cross, oblong cross with backstitch, double leviathan, Rhodes, Scottish and knitting stitch (see stitches, page 145 and ff.).
For design diagrams, see pages 158–161.

Working comments

This design was worked free form, using the colours as a palette and choosing them, the stitch, and the thread to be used, as the work progressed. However some preliminary planning was necessary – in a design like this the range of colours and the types of thread to be used must be chosen before you begin. In this case, again, the centre motif was balanced by the outer border, and as the centre panel was composed of quite large rectangles and triangles in shades of green, the border was planned in the same colours and a bold stitch. A touch of silvery blue stranded cotton was added to lighten the effect a little. Once the centre panel was complete a deep border was worked around it, using different stitches and threads in the coral colours. To add interest it was then turned cornerwise and another border was worked diagonally, filling in the triangle left with Scottish stitch in the very pale coral background colour.

When you are using this freeform technique it is essential to work outwards from the centre panel, building up the first border row by row so that as each row adds a different texture and colour you can then decide what to use next to it. If, as we did with this cushion, you then decide to use another inner border, this should be worked next (after the centre panel). The two areas can then be united by a filler stitch in the background colour. Do *not* try to work separate small areas here and there over the canvas and then hope to unite them all at the end. Work borders to define each area and then fill in that section before moving on to your next border.

Above and left: the Bargello Velvet Sofa Cushion

THE BARGELLO VELVET SOFA CUSHION

The lovely glowing fabric used as the source for this design is based on the traditional Florentine or Bargello patterns. Of course, it would be easy simply to copy the pattern in stitches but, as there are already six cushions of that pattern on the sofa, why bother making one more? What follows is our own solution to the design challenge.

We decided first on a contrast to the square shapes of the original cushions, so we chose a circle. With the circle as the outline further curves were sketched in, along with diagonal and horizontal lines to break down the areas. Arcs and diagonals gave triangles and these emerged as tiny shapes at the focal point of the cushion.

This design is perhaps the most sophisticated in concept of the designs in this book and if you attempt to make something similar you will need to think freely about shapes and areas. It will be helpful to refer to your first lettering design (see page 41) where letters were used to break down areas into further abstract shapes.

Analysis

CANVAS No. 16 single mesh. Design size $10\frac{1}{2}$ in. (27 cm) circumference.

TEXTURES Strandable wool used as 1- and 2-ply, perlé and stranded cotton.

COLOURS *Wool:* medium amber No 4: medium blue/green No 4: medium dark blue/green No 5: medium sherry rose No 4: light beige No 2
Stranded cotton: light cream Anchor 0386: light beige Anchor 0388
Perlé: pale amber DMC 945: medium bright amber DMC 301: dark amber DMC 400: dark rose DMC 3328: light rose

DMC 760: light beige DMC 842: medium beige/brown
DMC 841: medium blue/green DMC 597: medium (bright)
green DMC 992

STITCHES   Flame, tent, cross, slanted Gobelin, brick (worked horizontally) (see stitches, page 145 and ff.).
For design diagrams, see pages 174–6.

Construction

The circle shape was sketched, then broken down with curved divisions and horizontal and diagonal dividing lines. The emergent shapes were then marked on the canvas. Remember that in needlepoint curves cannot always look symmetrical because of the slope of the stitches. While we kept to the Bargello patterns of the flame stitches we worked the separate areas from different angles – some horizontally and some vertically – to give a feeling of movement and to add interest. The background was worked in the light beige wool but the perlés and stranded cottons were used for the colours, sometimes just to tip the coloured wools with shine, and sometimes alone to capture the effect of the brilliance and shine of the velvet.

Working comments

The two curved bands were worked first using the main colours of the fabric. The cross bands were then established using the colours and working the small triangles at the centre. This left the larger areas which were worked at the contrasting angles and using the flame stitches at different levels and different slopes for added interest.

77

Overleaf left: the Art Nouveau Photograph Frame
Overleaf right: the Lime Green Spanish Cushion

THE LIME GREEN SPANISH CUSHION

This rug, though very simple in design, offered several different possibilities for a needlepoint adaptation. We particularly liked the geometric grid pattern so we took this for our theme, highlighting it in shiny threads in two areas and using rougher textures in the background areas that were in keeping with the textural feeling of the rug. The bright lime green borders set off the delicacy of the cream silk areas.

Alternatively we could have used the grid as a background for the whole design, with a central motif and a border, perhaps the leaves or an initial; or the grid could have been used as the border only and the lime-coloured borders brought into the centre – perhaps reversing the colours. However we chose the interesting asymmetric arrangement of the two grid sections.

Analysis

CANVAS   No. 16 single mesh. Design size $14\frac{1}{2} \times 10$ in. (37×25.25 cm).

TEXTURES   Wool, stranded cotton and perlé.

COLOURS   *Wool:* light cream beige No 2: bright/medium lemon yellow No 4: medium yellow/green No 4: dark olive green No 6
Stranded cotton: dark olive green Anchor 0845
Perlé: pale cream DMC 712: light lime green DMC 3348: medium leaf green DMC 471

STITCHES   Tent, brick (worked horizontally), Scottish, slanted Gobelin, double leviathan (see stitches, page 145 and ff.).
For design diagrams, see pages 168 and 169.

80

Construction

In this case we decided to use double leviathan stitch for the squares, with tent stitch dividing lines. Once this was decided we could establish the size of the two areas and mark them on the canvas – each stitch is four threads and each tent stitch covers one thread. We marked the canvas accurately into the two rectangular inner areas and an outer edge was also drawn on the canvas. The tent stitch outlines were worked first and filled in with the large double leviathan stitches. The heavy borders in slanted Gobelin stitch were worked around the grid areas first and then around the outer edges. Then scattered double leviathan stitches in wool, boxed in perlé tent stitches, were worked in the background area. This was then filled in using brick stitch worked horizontally.

Working comments

This design was so easy to work and its choice of colours and stitches was limited and simple. The raised textures of the double leviathan stitches worked in perlé in the grids gave a sleek contrast with the rougher texture of the double leviathan stitches in the woollen background areas – in keeping with the rough woollen texture of the rug. We used the dull beige/cream colour for this area to contrast sharply with the clear shiny colour of the cream perlé and also to cool down the brightness of the citron yellow wool. A clearer cream colour would have been too bright.

The Lime Green Spanish Cushion

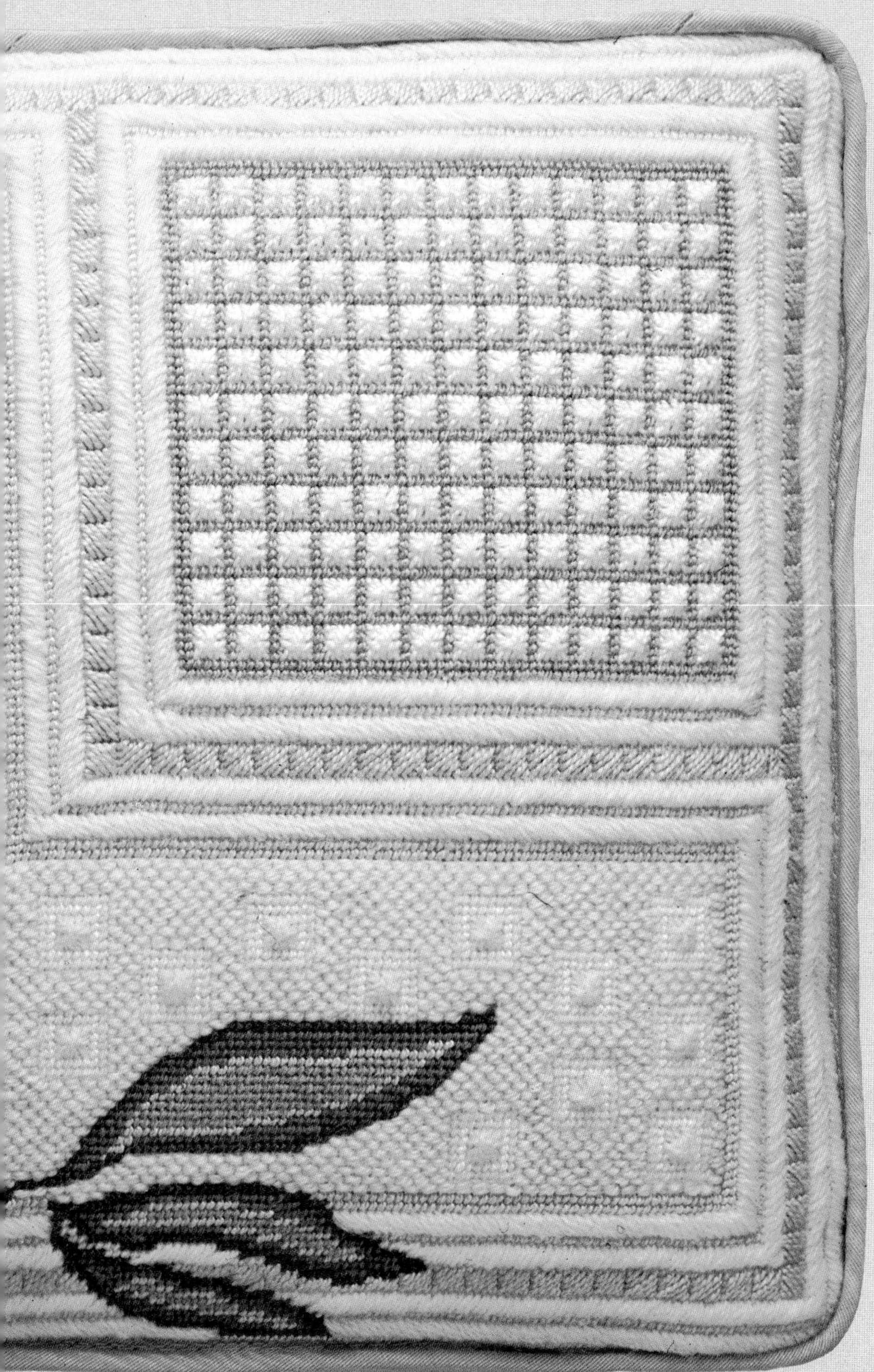

THE ICED PINK MOIRÉ SILK CUSHION

The shimmering iced colour of pale moiré silk fabric, combined with its shine and the uneven woven texture, were the sources for this design and also for the turquoise blue design which follows. There is, of course, no printed fabric pattern to use here as a theme. Instead the designs are an abstract expression of the textural and colour qualities of the fabric. So if you have used plain fabrics in your rooms these two designs may help you to see them afresh as a basis for a needlepoint design.

Analysis

CANVAS No. 16 single mesh. Design size 10 × 10 in. (25 × 25 cm).

TEXTURES Strandable wool, stranded cotton, and perlé.

COLOURS *Wool:* dark true pink No 6: light iced pink No 2: light butter yellow No 2: pale lemon yellow No 1: medium avocado green No 4
Stranded cotton: pale pink DMC 225: light butter yellow DMC 472
Perlé: dark raspberry pink DMC 335: medium raspberry pink DMC 899: light raspberry pink DMC 776: light green DMC 472

STITCHES Tent, leaf, cross, upright Gobelin, double leviathan and brick (see stitches, page 145 and ff.)
For design diagram, see page 166.

Construction

We decided that both the pink and the turquoise blue designs would be made up of a centre panel and a border, but in the pink one the border would use the fabric as its theme with the centre panel as a contrasting motif, whilst in the blue the centre panel would use the source fabric pattern and the border would be the decorative motif.

The first step was to construct the octagon (see techniques, page 30), mark it on the canvas and indicate the centre point. We chose to use stranded cottons and perlés for their shine and texture, in deeper pink colours than the fabric so that we would have a contrast. The wools for the octagonal panel were chosen in paler colours closer to the tone of the fabric.

The centre motif of leaf stitches was worked first and then the octagonal border, establishing it row by row for texture, stitch and colour as described for the bamboo cushion (number three in the Peony Garden series) on page 72. The four outer corner panels were worked in the pink perlés and stranded cottons in a simple Bargello stitch to capture the ribbed shine of the fabric.

Working comments

The large background area of the octagonal panel needed a textural contrast, and we used the subtle change of colour (butter yellow in the same tone value as the pink background colour) with a different texture, (stranded cotton) and a large squared off stitch, to break the area (see diagram). It is important to use very close colour tones in this case or you will get a spotted effect rather than a textural one, but the change of colour is far more effective than just a simple change of stitch, and is still understated enough not to detract from a main design theme. It is a very useful device for making large areas of background interesting.

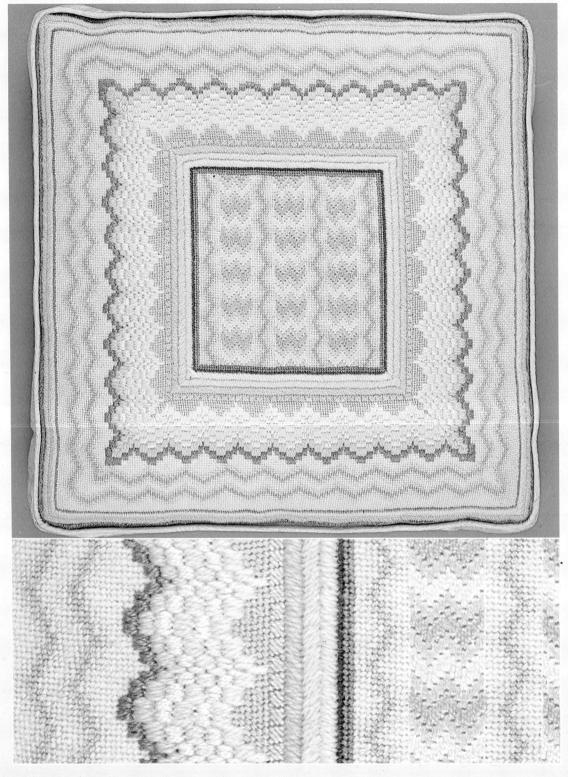

The Iced Blue Moiré Silk Cushion

The Iced Pink Moiré Silk Cushion

THE ICED BLUE MOIRÉ SILK CUSHION

Although we were using the same moiré silk as the source for this design – this time in the pale turquoise blue – we wanted to achieve a very different effect, heavier and more patterned. This time we took the centre panel from the fabric and added a decorative border.

Analysis

CANVAS   No. 16 single mesh. Design size 15 × 15 in. (38 × 38 cm).

TEXTURES   Strandable wool split to 1- or 2-ply (specified where used), stranded cotton and perlé, used two strands together.

COLOURS   *Wool:* pale turquoise blue No 1: light aquamarine No 2: medium aquamarine No 4
Stranded cotton: pale blue Anchor 0158: pale blue grey Anchor 0848
Perlé: light turquoise blue DMC 747: medium turquoise blue DMC 926: dark teal blue DMC 924: medium/light silver grey DMC 928

STITCHES   Flame, Bargello I-A, tent, slanted Gobelin, Scottish (see stitches, page 145 and ff.).
For design diagrams, see pages 162 and 163.

Construction

The centre panel and the outer edges were marked on the canvas. We worked the centre panel in alternate stripes of flame stitch and tent stitch, arranged in blocks of four and worked down the canvas to give a wavy effect (see diagram). A strong border of slanted Gobelin stitch was then worked around this panel. The outer border was worked in the scalloped Bargello I-A pattern edged with the same tent stitch waves as in the centre panel. Wool was used 1 ply for tent stitch, and 2 ply for Bargello and slanted Gobelin.

Working comments

The corners of the outer border must be mitred and it is best to do this by working your first row almost to the corner point. Then work a row on the next side almost to meet this corner point. Then, keeping the sequence of the stitch, work them inwards to meet at the corner. Once the first corner row is established you simply repeat it (see diagram). However, none of the four corners is exactly alike and you would probably have to be a mathematician to achieve it when working freeform like this, particularly in the surrounding border of tent stitches where the corners could not be the same because the wavy pattern never meets at the same angle.

If perfect accuracy is what you are after it is possible to work out a design like this on graph paper first, but then you must plan out all the stitches that you will be using. It is a perfectly acceptable approach but we prefer the pleasure of working freely and letting the work grow organically with every stitch, thread and colour chosen. You are free to change your mind as you work and the design loses none of its charm for a little less geometric perfection.

Above: Anabelle's Rose Pink Cushion

Right: the Blue and Cream Lace Cushion

THE BLUE & CREAM LACE CUSHION

Anabelle's lace bedspread with its blue underlining was the source for this cushion, and to achieve a lacy effect in needlepoint to compliment the bedspread was the challenge. The lace of the bedspread is a rather coarse cotton weave and we therefore used the soft embroidery cotton in an ecru colour for its matte cotton appearance. So that the overall effect was not too soft, we chose shiny perlé for the background, giving the cushion a delicate quality and emphasizing the lacelike effect.

Analysis

CANVAS   No. 18 single mesh. Design size $10\frac{1}{2} \times 10\frac{1}{2}$ in. (26.5 × 26.5 cm).

TEXTURES   Soft embroidery cotton and perlé.

COLOURS   *Soft embroidery cotton:* ecru DMC
Perlé: light Wedgwood blue DMC 800: medium Wedgwood blue DMC 799: dark (bright) Wedgwood blue DMC 792: light cream DMC 712

STITCHES   Leaf, cross, oblong cross with backstitch, tent, large diamond eyelet, small eyelet, upright Gobelin, and Bargello I-B and I-C (see stitches, page 145 and ff.).
For design diagrams, see pages 164 and 165.

Construction

Some preliminary marking of the canvas was necessary. Once the design size was established, the corner points and the centre point were marked. As the design was going to be basically geometric, we divided the square into quarters for easier reference when counting. An inner square $5\frac{1}{2} \times 5\frac{1}{2}$ in. (14×14 cm) was marked to establish a wide outer border. The scalloped edges of the lace pattern were counted out and marked on the canvas on the outside edge and on the inner square. The rest of the design evolved from these established points – that is, an outer and inner scalloped border and a centre point. Both these borders were worked first and expanded by alternating the blue with the ecru to form a triple row of scallops. From there we moved to the centre square and the pattern evolved starting from the eyelet stitch at the centre. We wanted to keep the pattern in the border bolder and less intricate and busy than in the centre so it was expanded using the leaf stitches. The final stitches were the bright blue perlé background cross stitches.

Working comments

It may sometimes be a bit difficult to keep all your cross stitches lined up neatly under each other when working freeform in a large background area that takes in a combination of other stitches. We suggest working all the stitches from one point rather than filling some in as you go along – for instance from the inside border outwards. This design was actually much less complex to work than it appears and you need not be afraid of attempting something as seemingly intricate. If you establish your counted borders first and use your own imagination and preferred stitches you will find it easier and more fun than trying to sew an exact copy of this one – and far more satisfying too.

Making up

As a finishing touch to this cushion we added a frill of lace as well as piping to accentuate the delicate, feminine feeling of the design.

The Green Initialled Cushion

The Art Nouveau Photograph Frame

THE GREEN INITIALLED CUSHION

This design was also inspired by a lamp with its soft green colour and geometric bamboo borders. When the shapes were sketched roughly we saw that they formed interesting interlocking corners. As before, we chose not to use the small flower pattern. The bold border became the most important part of the design and the centre panel was a secondary motif which emerged from the shape of the flame stitch borders – and which suited our 'A' initial perfectly. The colour of the lamp reminded us of the iris in bloom in the garden, the soft purples and silvery greens and the stronger apple greens of that time of year, and suggested to us the contrast colour of soft violet.

Analysis

CANVAS   No. 16 single mesh. Design size 15 × 11 in. (38 × 28 cm).

TEXTURES   Strandable wool split to 2-ply, stranded cotton and perlé.

COLOURS   *Wool:* pale iris No 1: light iced green No 2: pale lemon yellow No 1
Stranded cotton: light cream/yellow Anchor 0386
Perlé: pale lilac DMC 211: medium violet DMC 209: dark violet DMC 208: medium pink/mauve DMC 554: light silver green DMC 928: light apple green DMC 369

STITCHES   Flame, tent, oblong cross with backstitch, double leviathan see stitches, page 145 and ff.).
For design diagrams, see pages 172 and 173.

Construction

The bamboo borders were sketched and then re-drawn to make them symmetrical. They were then counted out onto the canvas (it is worth taking the time and trouble to do the counting, and make sure that the borders are quite even. It causes more work later if you find you are a couple of stitches off. Unpicking is not fun!). The outer border strips were worked first and filled in solidly. The border was expanded outwards and then inwards using flame stitches and alternating texture and colour to form a pattern. This left a small centre panel where we decided to put an initial A, and this was further embellished at the bottom with more flame stitches which fitted nicely into the base of the letter. A small extra pattern of flame stitches was put in the centre of the A.

Once again, the completed design looks complicated, but if you follow the working plan and the way it all evolved you will see that it was quite logical and simple. As always, all you need is a starting off point, and that you get from your source or theme.

A very important point to watch when working flame stitch, as with the inner borders here, is that it must be worked row by row all around the four edges, *not* by working the whole of one side first and then the next. Working it right round enables you to mitre the corners neatly by joining them as you go along (see diagram). The A was worked horizontally for a neater effect and it was easier to shade it that way. The surrounding panel of tent stitch was worked in 1-ply wool.

WORKING SEQUENCE

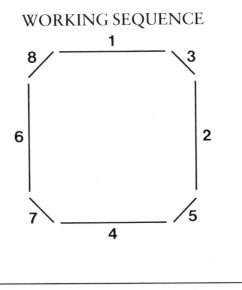

97

Overleaf: Richard and Elizabeth Adler with some of their needlepoint cushions

Two Photograph Frames
WITH AN ART NOUVEAU THEME

Here are two very different interpretations of the same design. One photograph frame is worked in needlepoint, the other introduces the crystalline effect of beading. The source for the two designs was a typical art nouveau pattern, well known to all of us. We are surrounded by references for art nouveau, the most familiar being the William Morris designs, but there is no need to be limited to these. Look out for suitable themes in reference books in the libraries and in the shops.

Analysis

CANVAS
No. 18 single mesh. Design size outer edge $9\frac{1}{2} \times 7\frac{1}{2}$ in. (24×19 cm), inner edge $4\frac{1}{2} \times 3\frac{1}{2}$ in. (11.5×9 cm).

TEXTURES
Strandable wool used split to 1-ply, stranded cotton and perlé.

COLOURS
Wool: medium blackberry No 4
Stranded cotton: medium/dark pink/mauve DMC 3041: medium rose Anchor 066: light lilac Anchor 018: dark forest green Anchor 0860: medium willow green Anchor 0842: light willow green Anchor 0843: light silver green Anchor 0858
Perlé: light willow green DMC 503: medium/dark willow green DMC 501: light apple green DMC 369: medium/dark pink/mauve DMC 316

STITCHES
Tent, Scottish, cross (see stitches, page 145 and ff.).
For design diagrams, see pages 170 and 171.

Construction

Colour must be handled carefully in a picture frame because it must not be allowed to dominate the photograph it is to enclose. This doesn't mean that it need lack colour, only that the colours should be kept delicate and a little subdued. Most photographs to be framed will have colours of their own – probably the strong blues of summer seas or the bright greens of gardens. Even if you are planning to frame a black and white picture, try not to make the colours too bold. You are working in a very small area and must keep in mind the contrast of the picture with its frame. Similarly, the design of the frame should itself be not too 'busy' so as not to overwhelm its subject.

This design was drawn out on the canvas first, and was then worked entirely in tent stitch using the shiny threads for the leaf design, and the wool, used as one strand, for the main background area. Once the design panel was established the frame was embellished at the edges and corners using different threads and stitches for extra definition. These all evolved as the work progressed and were not established initially.

Working comments

The canvas most suitable for these small items is the no. 18 single mesh, which gives the small stitch necessary for the very small area and detail required. Using single mesh canvas it is quite easy to see and to work, but remember that when you are using wool only one strand is necessary. The stranded cotton was used unsplit. Number 5 perlé works well on this size canvas.

Overleaf right: Blue and Cream Lace Cushion

THE BEADED FRAME

The frame is completely beaded, but beads can also be used in combination with your needlepoint either at random to give a sparkly effect, or in groups for added density or to provide a contrast. They look lovely in frames and wall hangings, but bear in mind that they can be rather impractical for cushions – even the large wooden beads – as they tend to catch on clothes when people sit or lean against them (and we hope that all your cushions will be in use, not kept to be admired from afar).

This frame was worked for us by Diana Keay, a marvellously knowledgeable lady who is also one of the best and most respected teachers of needlepoint in Britain.

Analysis

MATERIALS: Number 10 double mesh canvas. (Double mesh canvas is usually used for beaded designs as we use *all* the threads, as in petit point, attaching a bead to each one. This gives a closely covered uniform surface using small beads. Number 10 mesh is a good size for the type of small bead we have used.)

A packet of beading needles

Ordinary sewing cotton

Small brilliant beads large enough to cover the mesh of the canvas.

Construction

The design is first drawn out on the canvas, using an indelible marker pen. The beads are applied in rows, working from left to right and fastening off securely at the end of each row. The stitch used is exactly like the tent – the needle is brought up from the back of the canvas, threaded through the bead and taken back to the wrong side again (see diagram). Any ordinary strong sewing thread (e.g. Sylko) is suitable.

A second method using couching is better for larger areas – it covers equally well and is faster. The beads are first strung onto the thread which is laid across the surface and then secured with couching stitches (see diagram).

When the beading is complete, two rows of tent stitch should be worked around both the inside and the outside edges of the frame so that there is room to stretch the work neatly over the frame support.

Working comments

Beading is quite simple to do, but take care to arrange the beads neatly.

The whole of this frame was beaded to show you the effect, but you could try any other combination of beads and stitchery. You could perhaps work the design in beads and the background in needlepoint, or the borders only in beads. Random beading can be a most attractive way to add a little sparkle or frosting. See page 40 in the techniques chapter for how to make up the frame.

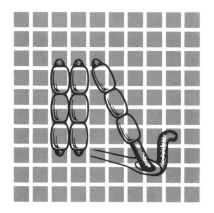
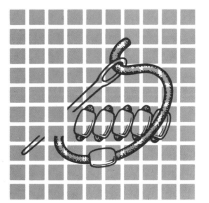

Detail of the Green Initialled Cushion

Anabelle's original drawing for Belle's Ice-Cream

Anabelle's Rose Pink Cushion

A lamp with an unusually shaped bamboo pattern border was the starting point for this design. We decided that the flower pattern, while very pretty, was too insignificant and small for needlepoint and so we simply adapted the borders to frame our daughter's name. The pink colour of the lamp was used and a muted medium tone of teal blue chosen as a contrast and to subdue the pinks a little, along with a very pale creamy pink.

Analysis

CANVAS
No. 16 single mesh. Design size 12 × 11 in. (30.5 × 28 cm).

TEXTURES
Strandable wool split to 2-ply, stranded cotton and perlé.

COLOURS
Wool: light duck egg blue No 2: light aquamarine No 2
Stranded cotton: pale cream/pink DMC 819
Perlé: medium/dark teal blue DMC 926: light turquoise blue DMC 747: medium raspberry pink DMC 3350: light fondant pink DMC 818

STITCHES
Brick, tent, double leviathan, knitting, slanted Gobelin (see stitches, page 145 and ff.).
For design diagram, see page 176.

Construction

A preliminary sketch of the shape of the bamboo borders was made. To achieve the neat geometric effect we were after it was necessary to count this out over the mesh of the canvas and then mark it with an indelible marker pen. A style of lettering for the name was decided upon and this was also counted out and marked onto the canvas (see pages 44–45 for further details about lettering). It is a good idea to work letters out on graph paper first.

As the borders really came first in this design, they were worked first. The effect we wanted was that of strips of shiny silk braid or ribbons, so we used the stranded cottons and perlés to give the right texture. The straight edges of the borders were worked first and the corners were worked last, fitting the stitches into the shapes that we had and filling in with tent stitch. Once again the corners are not all identical because of the different angles, although they are the same size and contain the same number of threads. The name was worked next and mounted on a panel of tent stitches. The three background areas (around the name panel and on the top and bottom borders) were worked in the two muted blue wools to contrast with the shiny border and centre panel and again the boxed double leviathan stitches added interest to the background areas.

Working comments

When you are working repeated rows of a bold stitch like the double leviathan, you will find that they look better if they are lined up neatly under each other. In this design, as each succeeding row in the border became a bit longer, we often ended up with a bit over – e.g. two threads where four were needed. In this case you could simply work half a stitch, or, if you prefer, fill in with tent stitch using the same thread and colour. When working the diagonal strips at the corners the same principle is followed. The crossbands at the top of the corners were simply the logical outcome of the continuous placing of the double leviathan stitches and did not involve any complex counting. The gaps left were filled in with tent stitch in the contrasting colour and made nice little decorative triangles. The type of angular lettering we used for the name works well in needlepoint where curves are always a problem, and again we filled in with tent stitch where there was no room for the slanted Gobelin stitch.

Most of the designs we have shown you in this book are cushions, for the simple reason that designing a cushion is the most straightforward way of exploring the colour and design influences surrounding you in your home. Of course, needlepoint projects need not focus on something that is to be 'part of the decor' like a decorative cushion. As you can see from Anabelle's designs on pages 126–133, certain graphic subjects lend themselves perfectly to being framed and hung on the wall – quite different from the colour- and texture-dominated pieces that we have already described and which were inspired by fabrics or other patterned sources. To go even further, some designs cry out for a three-dimensional interpretation – and we'd like to illustrate this rather different approach with our doorstop designs.

The Pepsi Brick

The doorstops

In our introduction, we mentioned a series of needlepoint doorsteps that we designed a little while ago. The idea was to reproduce familiar, graphic labels in the unfamiliar medium of needlepoint. It's an amusing idea, like a one-line joke in stitches, and open to all kinds of experimenting. The original suggestion for the doorstops (they can also be used as paperweights or bookends) came from a *Times* journalist who loves needlepoint and was discussing, as were the rest of the British media at the time, the purchase by the Tate Gallery of the controversial *Pile of Bricks*. She thought that we should take our own pile of bricks and cover them with needlepoint, making a rather more colourful work of art of our own. So we went ahead and designed a brick cover with *The Times* logo, and other well-known graphic images followed on – the American eagle, and a bar of Cadbury's chocolate among them.

The Harrods Parcel

There are two of these designs that we particularly like; the first a Harrods parcel with the shop's famous logo, and the other based on the Pepsi-Cola logo and an unusual advertising slogan. The Harrods parcel had to be three-dimensional, of course, and in the Pepsi design we were able to incorporate a series of references to the same theme on the various faces of the brick shape (we could, of course, equally well have chosen a cube or any other handy shape).

When you are planning any three-dimensional work like this you must start by considering the shape you plan to cover. In other words, first choose your brick – they come in varying sizes and a British standard brick is different from an American one. Then, as real bricks tend to shed bits of red grit, our next step was to cover ours in corrugated cardboard to create a more uniform surface and compensate for the various indentations in the brick itself. Once this is done, the brick or other shape can be measured. We tend to add 'a bit here and there' to compensate for the canvas having to be bent around the corners of the brick, and in the case of the Harrods and Pepsi bricks came up with the dimensions $9 \times 4\frac{3}{4} \times 3$ in. ($23 \times 12 \times 7.5$ cm).

In the case of the Harrods parcel, we wanted to emphasize the instantly recognizable name and lettering, and to finish it off with a ribbon bow to make the shape look like a package. In the planning we took care to allow for the final position of the images when moulded into their three-dimensional finished shape – 'Harrods' on the top and sides, just an 'H' on the short side flaps. We made sure that the ribbon would meet up accurately when the sides were stitched together, and then painted the finished design on to the canvas.

With the Pepsi brick, Anabelle liked the current Pepsi television commercial with a catchy jingle that went 'lipsmackinthirstquenchin . . .', so we planned the design so that the long message would run continuously round the sides of the brick, with the logo on the upper face. With a series of words like this, much more planning is necessary at the design stage. This is where graph paper comes in handy because the spacing of the letters and the subsequent placing of the words around the four flap sides must be counted out with absolute accuracy.

We used a no. 12 white mono canvas to cover a brick the same size as the Harrods parcel, and worked out that the centre panel (the top of the brick) was 55 stitches wide by 109 long. We blocked this shape out on graph paper and added the four flap sections as for the Harrods parcel. It was relatively simple to fit in the Pepsi logo on the top, with its big areas of colour and only five geometric upper case letters. The words of the jingle were another matter, as we had first to standardize an alphabet that would fit into the available space. Then it took quite a lot of counting and juggling about to find the right combination of letters and spaces to fit the dimensions – impossible to do without that great ally, graph paper. But a pencil and a rubber, together with a lot of patience and, at times, something a little stronger to go into your Pepsi, are all you really need to translate any suitable motif into an entertaining three-dimensional design.

Incidentally, to go with the Pepsi brick we also made a Diet Pepsi cushion, using the logo, the red, white and blue colours and a big, strategically-placed zip – very effective.

To make up your doorstop when the stitching is finished, sew the corners securely (the stitches should cover two rows of unworked canvas) into a neat brick shape. Trim the canvas one inch (2.5 cm) from the edge of the work. Do any last-minute padding that may be necessary to make the brick fit snugly inside its needlepoint cover, insert the brick and glue the remaining excess canvas to the bottom of the brick. Glue a piece of felt to the bottom of the brick to make a neat, non-scratch base.

These doorstops do, of course, make terrific presents with just the right, carefully-chosen motif – whether it is a brand name, a slogan, or anything else that has a special significance for the recipient. Just choose your subject, select your shape and sketch the design out on paper (graph paper for any design that is not absolutely simple). The brick inside isn't essential, although it adds the weight that makes the object functional as well as decorative. We did some designs using polystyrene which is tough, light and cuttable into almost any shape you like, and has the added advantage of being regularly discarded from the packing cases of large appliances. Whatever inner shape or material you are using, just make sure that you do all your measuring and calculating very carefully before committing anything to the canvas.

The choice of canvas depends on how simple the design is and how much detail will be required to execute your design satisfactorily. For the

The Overthorpe Hall Tapestry

Harrods parcel we used a no. 10 interlock canvas, as the ribbon and the lettering were both simple and straightforward, needing little detail. If we were contemplating a design that required more detail we would use a no. 14 mono canvas, and if we wanted to achieve a very realistic *trompe l'oeil* effect (perhaps a piece of jewellery inside a jewellery box – the box in the shape of the brick – to be given as a present instead of the real thing) then we would use a no. 10 or 12 Penelope canvas and would work the jewel and any other detail in petit point (20 or 24 stitches to the inch) and the background in gros point (10 or 12 to the inch).

Remember that you have a little leeway in measurement in that you can wrap your inner shape with as much corrugated paper as is necessary to fill your needlepoint cover snugly. So better to make your cover too big than too small . . . .

Working comments
To ensure that the stitches follow the same direction around the sides of the brick when it is eventually made up, work the main body of your design in the usual way from right to left. But turn your canvas around and work the two small end flaps as separate pieces, also from right to left.

TAPESTRIES & WALLHANGINGS

So far, we have talked about small, domestic projects for the home – pretty, decorative things that we hope will express your own taste and reflect your own surroundings.

But needlepoint does, of course, have much broader and more 'serious' applications; it is an art form in its own right with a long and splendid history. Any serious discussion of needlepoint as a 'pure' medium for creating modern tapestries or wallhangings is not the theme of this book, but no-one who does needlepoint at any level should be unaware of the artistic potentialities of the medium.

One method that we have used to create a large tapestry was with the children of Overthorpe Hall School, where each individual contributed a small square related to a uniting general theme (see page 135 and ff.), but the majority of large tapestry projects are by one designer with one theme – a concept much bigger in scope than anything we have looked at so far. It is impossible to give specific advice here, or even anything more than the most general of guidelines, but if you are thinking big a few hints may be useful.

Part of our work is the designing of large, 'monumental' tapestries for public buildings, and our major consideration is that the finished piece must harmonize with the architecture surrounding it. The setting always makes certain demands and imposes restrictions, and the tapestry has to be conceived with these in mind. This is no less true, of course, of any needlework project, whether it is for a footstool, a sofa or the entire wall of a hotel foyer. The area it is to cover, the colours and textures surrounding it and the play of light on it should all be considered when you conceive your design, whether its home is to be an office, a drawing room, a boat or a bedroom. It is just that with a large project the problems and demands are larger too. But remember, as you make your plans, that limitations – lack of light, starkness of surroundings or whatever they are – can also serve as real stimuli in helping you to create the perfect design for the particular location. A framework is necessary for any design, and the demands of its future setting should be one of the prime sources of inspiration.

One of the main difficulties in designing bigger pieces of work is the scale. The finished size must be in your mind from the very outset – it is no good at all to draw a design and then just enlarge it until it covers the right amount of space. The balance may look just right in a scale drawing one quarter or one half finished size, but proportions have a habit of changing strangely when the work is enlarged. Try to work out the layout on a piece of paper the same size as the finished design. Graph paper is best if the design has geometric elements, and a geometric approach at this construction stage is very helpful. The harmony of shapes that balance, or even parts of the design that 'work against' this balance, can be created through the division of areas into squares, circles, rectangles, triangles and so on.

Meticulous pre-planning is essential. Once you have created an arrangement of shapes and spaces that pleases you (in exactly the same way as in the first lettering project described on pages 43-8 – designing, on however grand a scale, still involves juggling shapes until they fall perfectly into place) it must be laid out on the paper with great care. Indicate all the areas of colour, textures and stitches before you begin. When you are working on a large scale it is all too easy to lose touch with the unity of the design. Of course there is scope for change and development as the work progresses so long as there is an original scheme to refer back to; new ideas will occur as textures and colours follow each other. Mistakes are inevitable, but through trial and error your creative 'eye' will become steadily more sophisticated.

Designing and working on a large scale is taxing, but there is nothing more stimulating than the scope and freedom 'pure' creativity offers.

DESIGNING
WITH CHILDREN

A child's needlepoint of view.

Mice, Anabelle's first design

Jumping Cats

Our daughter Anabelle has watched us do needlepoint ever since she was a baby, and even when she was only two years old she was interested in her mother's needlepoint projects. Canvas and wools were already part of her life when we decided to teach her how to design and work her own projects in the simplest way possible. Since then she has made some beautiful, personal things – and even did some designs for a series of commercial kits that we produced.

We all know that children draw a lot, and often come home from school or playgroup proudly clutching the latest artistic masterpiece. Take a fresh look at some of these drawings – from a needlepoint of view – and you will see that those gorgeous, scrawly pictures of 'Mummy and Daddy' could be worked with enduring charm onto canvas. We started doing this with Anabelle's drawings, and her delight at seeing her work of art in wools and stitches was an extra incentive to make her want to begin doing needlepoint herself. Childish pictures like this are easily transferred to canvas and are so easy to sew – but if your child is too young yet to do the stitching himself or herself, keep him or her involved and stimulate his interest by showing him each step as you do it.

Whether or not the child is going to do the actual sewing, your supervision is necessary in selecting and editing the drawings to be worked. As we found with Anabelle, often what you find most endearing and charming he will feel is 'not good enough' or 'too babyish' – and he may go away and draw something specially for the canvas which will have become much less free. For this reason it is usually better not to have your child 'design' something for needlepoint. Just watch his output at school and at home and you will usually find something with enough graphic simplicity to transfer easily onto canvas – and which has a special meaning both to your child and to you. Look out for the 'fantasy' pictures rather than the more figurative ones.

Please never try to add anything, except a border, to your child's designs – no shading or more realistic adjustment of colours. The charm is in the way he sees things. For example, anyone who has ever eaten an American ice-cream sundae will know just what Anabelle means by the fantasy of colour, froth, shine and size in 'Belle's Ice-Cream' on pages 130 and 133. As soon as she was old enough to sew, we used the following method to teach Anabelle to work her own designs.

The child does a drawing on paper using any familiar materials –
crayons, paints, marker pens or coloured pencils are perfect. When the
drawing is completed, take a piece of canvas (for a child, no. 10 mesh is
good, but for the very young, say under sevens, an even larger mesh like
no. 7 is easier to control) and put it over the drawing. Have the child trace
it on to the canvas, using permanent marker pens or acrylic paints (see
pages 31–2). It is quite easy to follow the lines of the drawing through the
holes in the canvas. At this design transfer stage, or even before, it is
important to introduce the wools used to work the design. Ideally, from
the beginning of the project, the child should have a colour chart of wools
as well as an assortment of yarns so that he learns to notice the colours
and textures of the threads. It is vital that he understands that although he
is using pens or paints now, these merely represent the colours of the
wools, and although he has done a drawing with paints he will later do
the same thing using wools and stitches. He will express himself in a new
medium, wools on canvas.

After the drawing has been completed the child should make the design
colour chart, in which he decides which colours of wool he intends to use
on his canvas. Each paint colour should be put on the chart, with a small
piece of the corresponding wool stapled to it and the number of the wool
shade for reference. This process teaches the child how to use a colour
chart, an important step in learning how to use colour, and immediately
takes him well beyond the childrens' packaged kits (which are usually
rather mediocre and not creatively stimulating). Once you have found a
brand of wools that you like, buy a colour chart of that company's wools
from your local retailer. It's a good investment as it is a handy reference
for colour ideas and provides a good colour education for the child – and
you! See the chapter on colour, page 53 and ff.

We have found that as the child gets older it is better *not* to colour in
the design on the canvas. Once he becomes familiar with the wools he
adopts a freer attitude to colour, often changing it as he sews. (Belle's Ice-
Cream, illustrated on page 130, changed from the drawing to the finished
canvas as she used each colour and then chose another to go next to it.)
Backgrounds need not be coloured in either unless the design has a very
dark background where the white canvas might show through a little.
(Children don't like to work on ecru or brown canvas. They prefer the

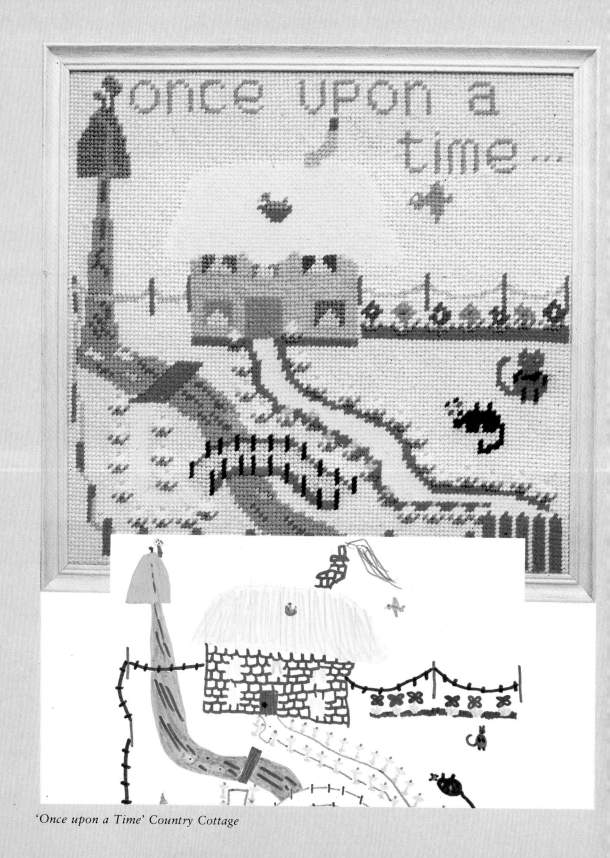

'Once upon a Time' Country Cottage

Dear Fido

soft black paws
furry smiling
faintest small tabby
striping
glossy furrer
gigantic purrer
halloween laughter
high grass scamper
bedtime curler
dear purrer
Sweet Fido

'Dear Fido'

more direct impact of colour on white.)

While this is going on the child should be taught to do tent stitch, and older ones can learn basketweave stitch as well. Most children can learn to do tent stitch with ease, and once they have one or two simple stitches in their repertoire it is easy to introduce more later to achieve added texture. The child then uses tent stitch to cover his painted design with the corresponding wool colour, making changes in colour or design as he sees fit as he goes along. At this stage the idea of *shading* can be introduced, the breakdown of one colour into different shades and depths. This usually immediately expands the child's understanding and use of colour. *Don't* try to influence the child's own colour choices. They will be naive and one-dimensional, and that is part of the charm. Too sophisticated a use of colour would be grafting adult ideas onto a childish theme and it would look quite wrong. Leave perspective and the relationship of larger objects to smaller ones up to the child, as their distorted proportions represent the child's view of the object's importance to *him*.

On the next pages are some examples of Anabelle's drawings, done between the ages of seven and eleven, and alongside them are the needlepoint pictures she made from them.

We used the methods given on the preceding page to help her to put them on canvas, and she sewed them herself (except that, in some of the earlier ones, we had to help out with the boring background bits!). The colours are her own choice, and you can see how each piece retains the fresh, naive quality of all children's drawings. Framed or made up into cushions they are cherished family reminders of her childhood.

MICE

Number 10 single mesh canvas using Coats tapestry wools and tent stitch. Design size $15 \times 9\frac{1}{2}$ in. (38×24 cm).

This was Anabelle's first design, done when she was seven years old. In fact as you can see, it emerged from a tiny drawing on a scrap of paper. At first only one mouse was going to be used on the canvas but then she amplified it with a second, slightly different mouse shape and then just a head. It worked beautifully – the only problem was the rather large background area. We helped her to transfer it onto canvas and she chose her colours. We showed her how to do tent stitch – and the mice were worked in a flash! Of course we ended up with the background to work for her – but the result is 'Mice' as only a child would see them – from a scrappy little drawing that might otherwise have been thrown away.

JUMPING CATS

Number 10 single mesh canvas using Coats tapestry wools and tent stitch. Design size 7×7 in. (18×18 cm).

This drawing, again done when she was seven years old, was inspired by one of Anabelle's cats who leaps three feet into the air seemingly at the drop of a pin. It captures the startled leap and the huge scared eyes so nicely, and again the childlike view of the tabby – with vertical stripes from paw to spine without a hint of a curve – is great fun.

Belle's Ice-Cream

Scuba Diver

'ONCE UPON A TIME' COUNTRY COTTAGE

Number 10 single mesh canvas using Coats tapestry wools and tent stitch. Design size 12 × 12½ in. (31 × 32 cm).

This is one of two designs that Anabelle did aged eight, illustrating the story opening 'Once Upon A Time'. The other one was a Fairy Tale Castle. The possibilities of this theme are infinite, of course, and it is a very good suggestion for a child in this age group to use as an idea for a picture which could be transferred to canvas. (There is enough fantasy in this simple phrase to stimulate most children's imagination.) This picture is the ideal storybook cottage, with a brook running down from the hills beyond and into the garden, a little bridge crossing it, the neat flowers, the plume of smoke from the chimney and of course, for Anabelle, two cats playing in the garden.

'DEAR FIDO'

Number 12 single mesh canvas using Coats tapestry wools and tent stitch. Design size 11¾ × 12½ in. (30 × 32 cm).

This poem was written by Anabelle when she was nine in memory of her first kitten, Fido, whose short life was filled with fun and mischief and affection. We worked out the letters on graph paper first and counted them onto the canvas and Anabelle added a border of simple flowers to frame the poem prettily.

132

BELLE'S ICE-CREAM

Number 14 single mesh canvas using strandable wool, stranded cotton and perlé and tent stitch, cross stitch. Design size 13 × 12 in (33 × 30.5 cm).

A marvellous eleven-year-old's fantasy ice-cream sundae – drawn after exposure to American ice-creams! This has a lovely freedom in the use of the ice-creamy colours used in shiny stripes in the sundae, picked up in toning stripes in wool in the background, and repeated in shiny threads in the border. For the first time in this design Anabelle used different textures of threads combined with different stitches and made a clever use of the repeat of pattern, colour and texture of thread – in true Adler fashion!

You will notice too that this time Anabelle deviated from her original coloured drawing and used the colours she had chosen in a much freer form, picking each one to compliment the one before as she went along.

SCUBA DIVER

Number 12 single mesh canvas using strandable wool used 2-ply and tent stitch, brick stitch and cross stitch. Design size $9\frac{1}{2} \times 7\frac{1}{2}$ in. (24 × 19 cm).

There is the beginning of a more sophisticated approach at this age, ten, first in the use of a slightly smaller mesh canvas for more detail, and secondly in the use of the different shades of blue in the sea for the different 'depths' of the water. But the nice touches of fantasy are still there in the pink snail and the striped fish. The wave shapes in three different colours are a graphic touch and the seaweed at the sides made an excellent natural frame. The detail of the design was worked in tent stitch, the background in brick stitch and a border was added using cross stitches in the sea colours.

THE OVERTHORPE HALL TAPESTRY

A large needlepoint tapestry, designed by a group
of children between the ages of six and eleven.

A GROUP PROJECT

Anabelle's friends have always been interested in the needlepoint projects they have seen scattered about our house, so it seemed a logical and attractive idea to involve all the children at her school in the designing and working of a large needlepoint tapestry. The staff at Overthorpe Hall – a small preparatory school for 150 pupils aged between four to twelve – was enthusiastic and work began in 1977. We were particularly lucky in having an understanding headmistress, Mrs Carduss, and a very creative craft teacher, Mrs Christie, to see the project through.

We and the staff felt that a uniting topic should be chosen which would inspire the children to create designs from the familiar world around them, so we decided upon the School, its Activities and Environment. 1977 was the year of the Queen's Silver Jubilee so the drawings often sprang from special activities and events that the children had enjoyed during the year.

As the first step, the teachers asked the children to make lists of potential subjects for designs under topics such as daily school activities, special activities and subjects, local birds, flowers, plants and animals. The basic topics were then discussed and each child chose an individual subject that interested her.

At this stage we made a design outline sketch of the whole project. We decided that a central rectangular panel, approximately 3 × 2 ft. (90 × 60 cm) depicting the school building, should be surrounded by a border of square panels of birds and flowers and animals and then another border of squares showing the activities of the school year. The whole would be enclosed by a plain border embellished with the name of the school and small flowers and insects. These last little motifs were to be undertaken by the smallest children who might not have been able to complete a whole design square, but who could certainly draw a spider or a ladybird. Once this plan was made, we were able to establish that the ideal size for the design squares was 10 in. (25 cm) – large enough for some detail yet small enough for a child to finish. Each child was provided with a piece of paper with a square of the right size drawn on it, and the drawing work began. (All the children were included, although the best results came from the six to eleven age group.)

Some subjects were drawn entirely from memory, such as Swimming, Gymnastics, the Jubilee Picnic, and Felling the Elms. Others needed source materials from natural history books. Each subject was treated individually and wherever the subject was available, such as mushrooms, plants and flowers in the school gardens, the child drew it from life.

They measured the school building, metrically, and used their powers of observation and analysis to put their subjects on to paper. The finished drawings were then put on display for all the school to see and the upper form gave an assembly talk explaining the Tapestry Project to the lower forms. The most suitable drawings were chosen to go into the tapestry, which had places for forty panels, and those children whose work had been picked proceeded to the next stage which was *putting the design on to the canvas.*

The canvas used was 10 to the inch white mono, cut and bound in 15 in. (37.5cm) squares.

The children used the usual method to transfer their drawings to canvas (see techniques, page 31). As the drawings were all in colour, the colours had to be indicated on the canvas too. (See painting on canvas, pages 31 and 32.)

Some subjects required more detail than others, and some children derived great pleasure from meticulously painting their canvases. Others just used the outline on their canvas as a basic guide and really enjoyed the creative process of working with the wool directly on the canvas.

Everyone learned tent stitch, including the staff. We adopted a standardized way of teaching the stitch so that the staff could oversee the work and point out any errors. Some of the children had to be taught how to thread a needle, and most of the youngest ones had to have this done for them at first.

It was an exciting moment when the wools arrived and the children were introduced to the beautiful colours.

Once the colours of the wools for each design had been chosen and related to the painted ones on the canvases, the stitching began. Most of the work was done in tent stitch, but some of the children learned basketweave stitch very quickly and this was used to fill in some of the background. It was fascinating to see how they used shades of colour to create visual interest, and how they learned to use the geometric structure of the canvas to create geometric shapes for the football net, the tennis net, library shelves, gymnastic bars and so on. They were never told *how* to shade, just introduced to the fact that they could use different coloured wools to vary effects just as they would with marker pens or paints.

The centre panel which was equivalent in size to eight squares became a group project, as it was too large for one child to do. When the child who had started to put the design on to canvas left for her next school the centre panel became a shared task. We worked on it, some children and the teaching staff all spent time working it, and as always the vast area of background became a shared chore. (As we had decided that the tapestry was to be done in basically one stitch we could not do much to make the background more interesting to work by introducing other textured stitches for the sky and garden.)

The strips for the border were left to the last as we all wanted to see how the panels looked next to each other, hoping that the effect would not be too much like a patchwork quilt or too busy in pattern. As we started to put the panels together on the floor we realized that we needed a border of one colour around each panel and an outer border in the same colour to unite the separated designs into a visual whole.

The muted green used in the borders was chosen by the staff to unite the tapestry with its 'home' in the old hall at the school. The alternative would have been to use a soft, true green in keeping with the childlike naive quality of the designs, which would have been appropriate to more modern surroundings.

Detail from the Overthorpe Hall Tapestry

(The wonderful thing about the use of colour, incidentally, is that the choice is vast and the decision personal. Many possible colours work equally well and the final choice conveys a definite personality to a project.) We decided on five rows of green on each side of the individual squares, which meant that the overall dimensions of the tapestry changed. The centre panel of the school needed to be made larger and the outer border needed to be expanded. (This situation comes up *often*, so if you miscalculate in any way accept it as part of the game and know that adjustments can almost always be made.)

When all the stitching was finished, each square, the centre panel and the border were blocked (see blocking and stretching, pages 33–6). We then had each panel sewn together with green wool, the extra canvas was cut away from each panel and the completed tapestry was backed with a cotton union fabric. The ideal way to join the sections of a large tapestry like this is explained on page 38.

The completed tapestry now hangs in the hall at the school and is an enduring memory of one school year.

The Overthorpe Hall Tapestry proves that even the very young can design and execute their own ideas in needlepoint, and can make a valuable contribution to a big and ambitious undertaking – even though they have never done a design of their own before or even seen a piece of canvas and a tapestry needle. Children – and adults – have more potential design talent than they think! All that is needed to get an exciting idea like this big group tapestry under way is one person who can coordinate, advise, and offer some basic information and encouragement like that provided in this book.

There are, of course, all sorts of people and places and events for which the creation of a needlepoint hanging would be the perfect celebration. For families, schools, villages or clubs the possibilities are endless, commemorating an anniversary or a centenary or a special achievement. As a group project like this is done in sections, it can be added to as you go along. Once the dimensions of the panels are standardized, it is possible for people in different places, even different countries, to contribute. And each individual, as at Overthorpe Hall, gains a real sense of personal achievement from having contributed to the finished work.

INDEX

Page numbers in italics indicate illustrations

STOCKISTS

Most of the materials used in this book are readily available from your local needlework stockist and department stores such as Liberty, John Lewis and Selfridges.

STITCH LIBRARY
AND
DESIGN DIAGRAMS

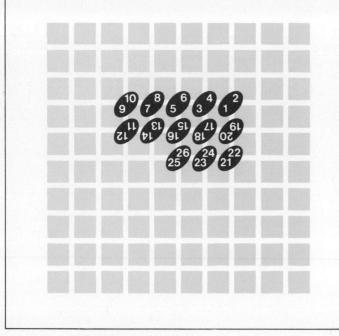

Right-handed method

1. Tent stitch (known as continental stitch in USA)

This stitch is essential for outlining, and for filling in small areas. Its advantages are that it is very easy to learn, and in conjunction with diagonal tent stitch (basket-weave) it can be used to fill an entire canvas, especially where working a picture-type design.

Its disadvantages are that it is time consuming because the canvas must be turned through 180° at the end of each row. It also distorts the canvas when used over large areas.

Left-handed method

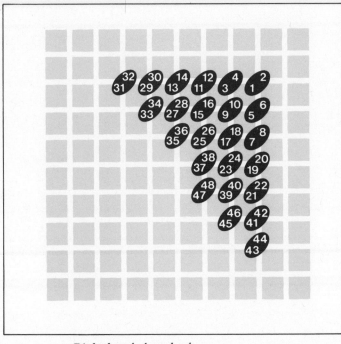

Right-handed method

2. Diagonal tent stitch (known as basketweave in USA)

This stitch presents the same surface appearance as tent stitch on the right side, but has a woven appearance on the back of the canvas (hence the name basketweave). It is an excellent stitch for filling in large areas. Its advantages are that it gives very little canvas distortion, is fast to work, and is very durable and firm. Its disadvantage is that it takes a little practice to learn the sequence of the stitches.

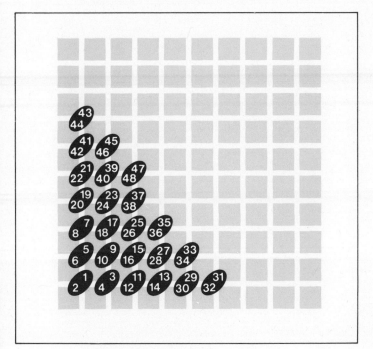

Left-handed method

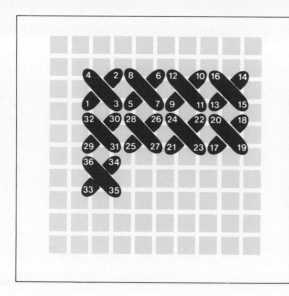

3. Cross stitch

The crosses must all go in the same direction. If you are using single mesh canvas, work each row stitch by stitch.

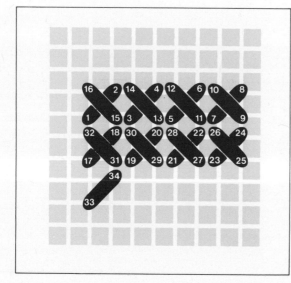

If using double mesh (Penelope) canvas, or interlocking (leno) canvas, first work the row of half cross stitches left to right then return, crossing them right to left.

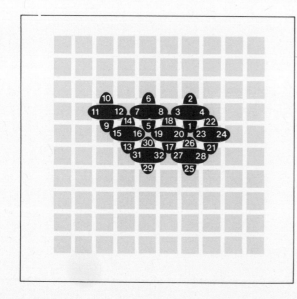

4. Upright cross stitch

This is a raised textured stitch which is quick and easy to work. Work each stitch individually and turn the canvas through 180° for the next row.

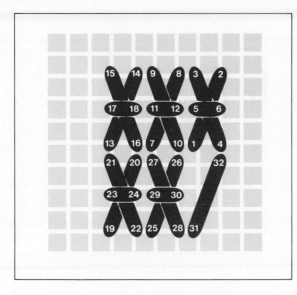

5. Oblong cross stitch with backstitch

A large and interesting stitch with raised texture, particularly effective used in borders. Work the stitch from bottom to top. It can also be used without the backstitch as a simple oblong cross stitch.

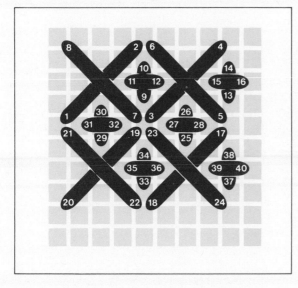

6. Double cross stitch

This stitch is actually two separate cross stitches – a large cross filled in with small upright crosses. It looks particularly interesting when worked in two colours.

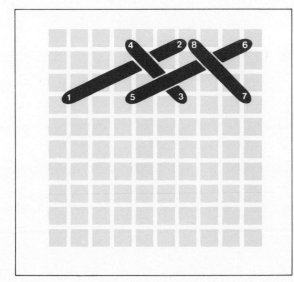

7. Long armed cross stitch

Another attractive cross stitch variation. Work it from left to right in horizontal rows.

149

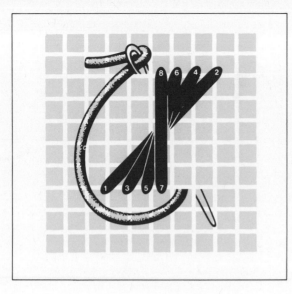

8. Rhodes stitch

This is the most complex-looking of the cross stitches but in fact it is very simple to work. Just follow the sequence. It is a very dominating stitch, larger and more raised than the double leviathan. Use it where a bold stitch is needed, for example in a large border or as a centre point. It is most effective worked in a perlé thread or stranded cotton as the shine captures the swirling movement of the stitch.

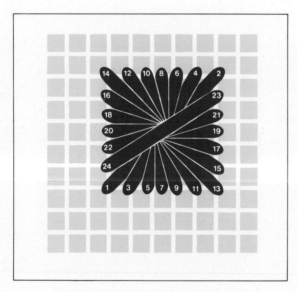

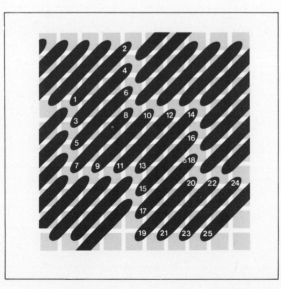

9. Byzantine stitch

This is another useful textured background stitch. Once the first row is established it is easy to repeat. It can also be worked in stripes of two or more colours, or shaded.

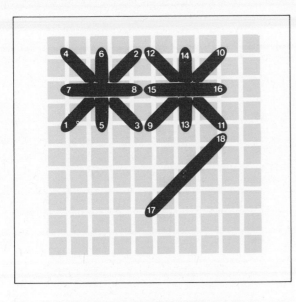

10. Smyrna cross stitch

A doubled-up cross stitch with a raised texture. Work each stitch individually and make sure they all cross in the same direction. Work horizontally from left to right.

11. Double leviathan stitch

A thick raised stitch, excellent for use in a border or as a corner or accent stitch. It is particularly effective worked in perlé or stranded cotton.

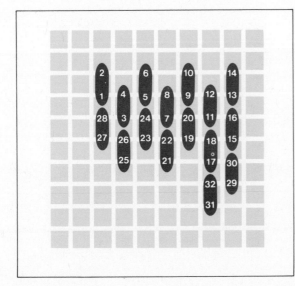

12. Brick stitch

This one is easy and quick to work, and is very useful as a background stitch. Work rows left to right and then right to left, without turning the canvas. To work horizontal brick stitch, simply turn the canvas on its side and work ordinary brick stitch.

151

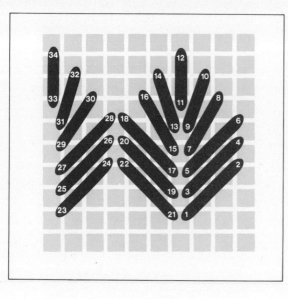

13. Leaf stitch

An attractive stitch that is useful in a border, but can also be used in large areas as a strong background stitch. Note that sequence 1–2 is repeated in 3–4 and 5–6. Next 7–8 moves in one hole at the top, and 11–12 moves in one more hole and is a straight stitch. The sequence is repeated on the other side working down from the top. Simply follow the numbers. The next stitch will connect at nos. 22, 20 and 18.

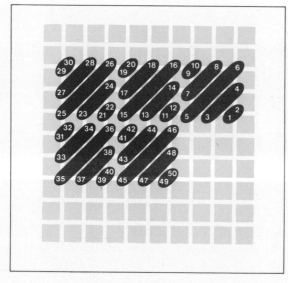

14. Scottish stitch

An excellent stitch when used for a background requiring more texture. It can be worked horizontally or diagonally. Do not pull thread too tight.

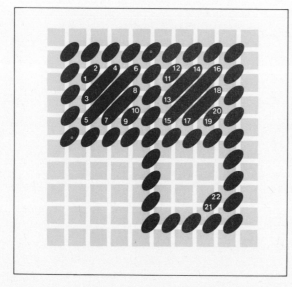

15. Scottish stitch with tent stitch

Each Scottish stitch is surrounded by boxes of tent stitches in the same colour to give a subtle variation in texture. Worked in two colours, it gives a checked effect.

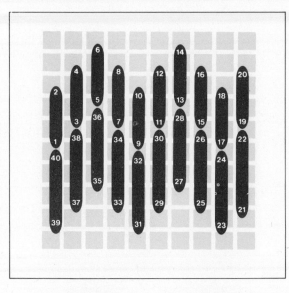

16. Flame stitch (Florentine or Bargello)

This stitch is worked over horizontal threads alternating row (1) over three threads and row (2) over four threads.

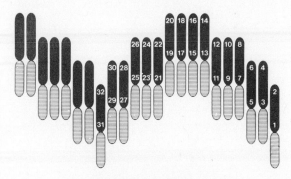

17. Bargello I (variations A, B and C)

Can be worked over two, three or four horizontal threads, or alternated. Very useful for borders. Bargello I-A is used in iced turquoise moiré silk design; Bargello I-B is used in blue lace design; Bargello I-C is used in blue lace design.

153

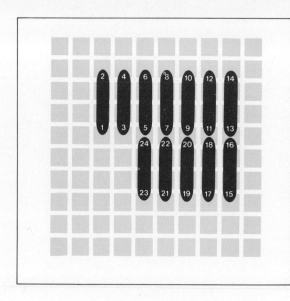

18. Upright Gobelin stitch

A vertical stitch which can be worked over two, three or four horizontal threads.

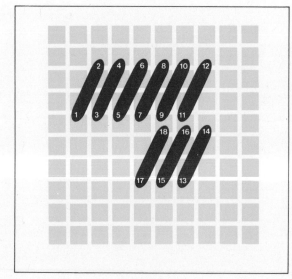

19. Slanted Gobelin stitch

This stitch is formed in the same way as upright Gobelin, but slanted to the right over one, two or three threads. To reverse the slope of the stitch begin from top left and work one, two or three threads to the right.

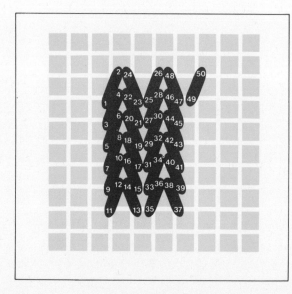

20. Knitting stitch

Worked vertically over two horizontal threads, sloping in one thread. If you want to work knitting stitch as a border, simply turn your work around so as to keep working horizontally.

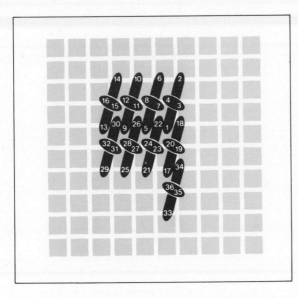

21. Knotted stitch

Worked over three horizontal threads slanted one thread to the right. It gives a neater appearance when each row is worked from right to left.

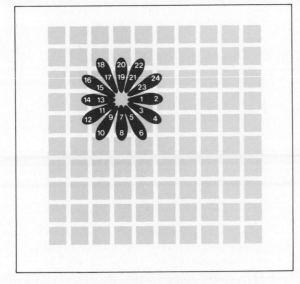

22. Eyelet stitch

A 'daisy' effect and very simple to work. A sequence of twelve stitches all worked from a centre point.

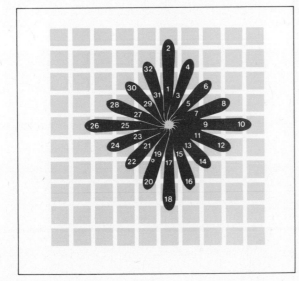

23. Diamond eyelet stitch

Recommended as a centre point only.

155

The Small Flower Cushion

this design uses wool only: work pattern and
background simultaneously, work borders last

background in brick
pale iced green

flowers in brick as
detailed right

156

Border

1 brick light/medium
   apple green
2 brick medium country
   green
3 upright cross light
   bronzed coral
4 upright cross
   light/medium bronzed
   coral

Flower Motif

1 brick medium country
   green
2 brick light/medium
   apple green
3 brick light/medium
   bronzed coral
4 brick light bronzed
   coral

The Peony Cushion

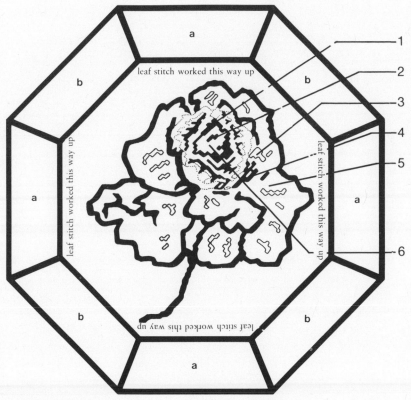

leaf stitch worked this way up

leaf stitch worked this way up

leaf stitch worked this way up

leaf stitch worked this way up

a

b

b

a

a

a

b

b

a

Flower Detail

1 cross medium/dark forest green SC
2 cross and tent light/medium apple green SC
3 accents in cross light silver green SC
4 *all* outlines in tent light/medium apple green SC
5 *all* petals in cross soft white wool (centres outlined in combination cross and tent in white SC)
6 *all* remaining centre in tent combination of light coral wool and medium coral SC

Border Detail

1 outline round edges cross light/medium paprika wool
2 leaf medium/dark forest green SC
3 leaf light/medium apple green SC
4 leaf light apple green wool
5 leaf medium apple green wool
6 leaf light silver green SC
7 upright cross light/medium apple green SC (all these panels are worked this way up)

Border Areas

a leaf (colours and textures detailed left)
b upright cross light/medium apple green

SC = Stranded cotton

background in brick light apple green wool

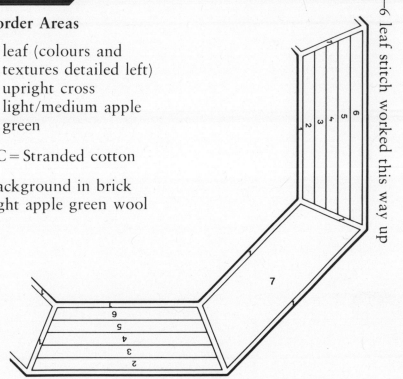

2–6 leaf stitch worked this way up

The Bamboo Cushion
Work Plan

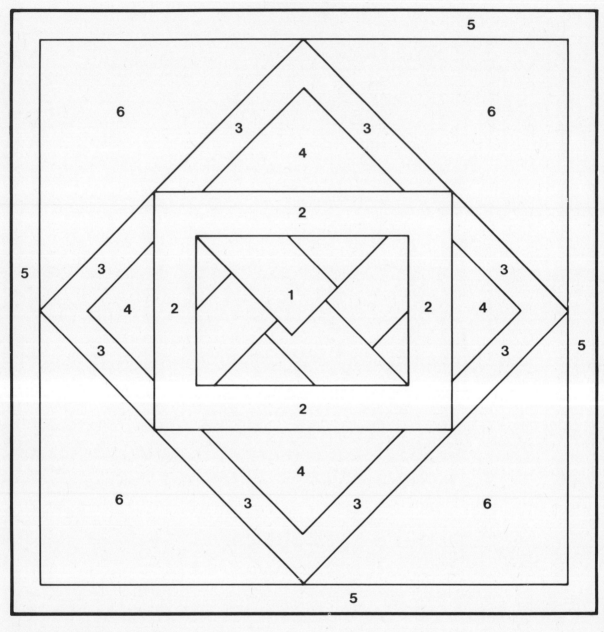

SC = stranded cotton

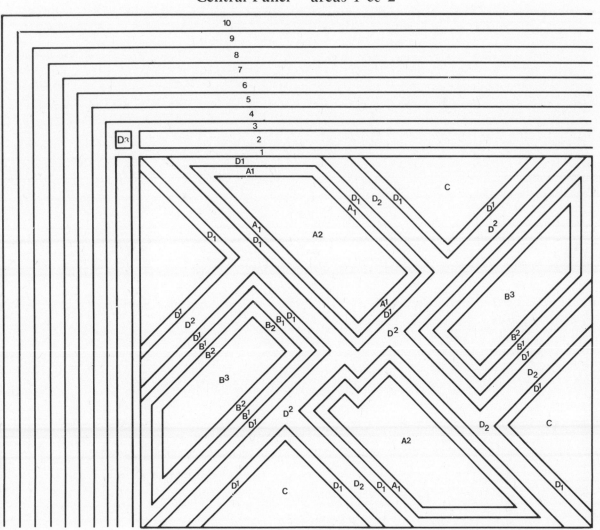

Area 1

A1 one row upright cross light silver blue SC

A2 brick light fiord green wool

B1 one row cross light silver blue SC

B2 two rows cross medium green SC

B3 cross light fiord green wool

C tent light fiord green wool

D1 tent medium coral perlé

D2 tent medium/dark green perlé

D3 in each corner, one double leviathan in medium/dark green perlé

Area 2

1 tent medium/dark green perlé

2 double leviathan medium coral perlé

3 tent medium/dark green perlé

4 cross medium/dark coral wool

5 tent medium coral wool

6 upright cross light coral wool

7 tent medium coral perlé

8 oblong cross pale coral wool

9 tent light silver blue SC

10 upright cross light fiord green wool

The Bamboo Cushion
Inner Panel – areas 3 & 4

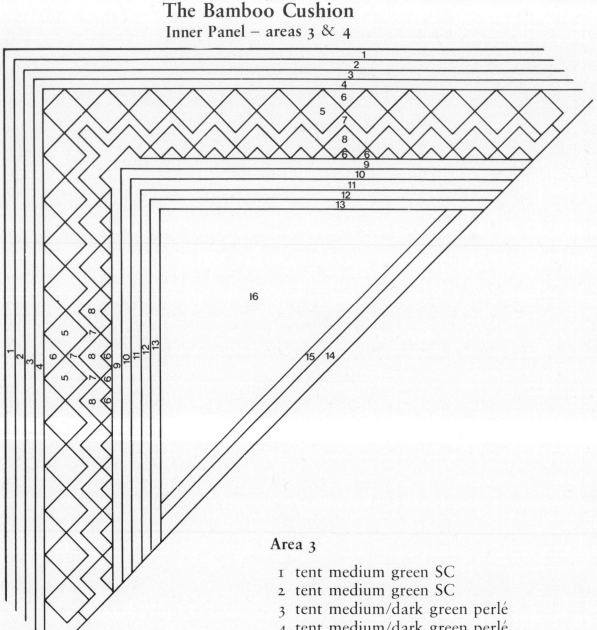

Work border from outer edge
inwards

Area 4

14 knitting medium coral perlé
15 tent light fiord green wool
16 Scottish pale coral wool

Area 3

1 tent medium green SC
2 tent medium green SC
3 tent medium/dark green perlé
4 tent medium/dark green perlé
5 double leviathan medium coral perlé
6 tent pale coral SC
7 tent medium/dark green perlé
8 & 9 upright cross medium/dark coral wool
10 tent pale coral wool
11 upright cross light turquoise blue wool
12 upright cross light silver blue SC
13 upright cross light fiord green wool

Outer Corners and Border – areas 5 & 6

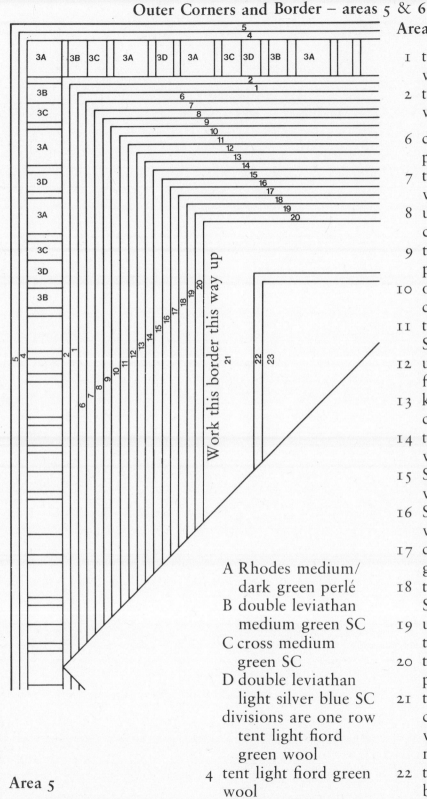

Area 6

1 tent light fiord green wool

2 tent light fiord green wool

6 cross medium coral perlé

7 tent medium coral wool

8 upright cross light coral wool

9 tent medium coral perlé

10 oblong cross pale coral wool

11 tent light silver blue SC

12 upright cross light fiord green wool

13 knitting medium coral perlé

14 tent light fiord green wool

15 Scottish pale coral wool

16 Scottish pale coral wool

17 cross light fiord green wool

18 tent light silver blue SC

19 upright cross light turquoise blue wool

20 tent medium coral perlé

21 three rows double cross in light coral wool, filled in with medium coral perlé

22 tent light turquoise blue wool

23 tent light fiord green wool

A Rhodes medium/ dark green perlé

B double leviathan medium green SC

C cross medium green SC

D double leviathan light silver blue SC

divisions are one row tent light fiord green wool

4 tent light fiord green wool

5 tent light fiord green wool

Area 5

3 band of alternating stitches:

The Iced Blue Moiré Silk Cushion

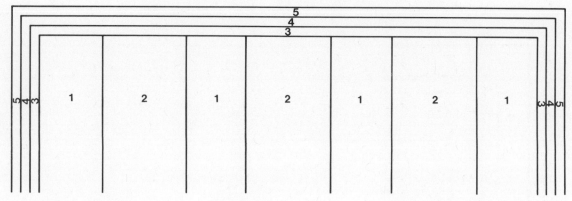

Central Panel

tent in blocks of four
to form wavy pattern
(see tent stitch detail)
2 flame alternating:
 light turquoise
 blue perlé (two
 strands)
 medium turquoise
 blue perlé
3 & 4 two rows tent
medium turquoise
blue perlé
5 tent dark teal blue
 perlé

Tent Stitch Detail

1 tent pale blue SC
2 tent medium turquoise
 blue perlé
3 tent pale blue SC
always work vertically

Flame Stitch Detail

all slanted Gobelin is
worked over two threads
1 slanted Gobelin (r to l)
 pale turquoise blue
 wool
2 slanted Gobelin (l to r)
 light aquamarine
 wool
3 slanted Gobelin (r to l)
 medium aquamarine
 wool
4 Scottish medium/light
 silver grey perlé
5 Bargello I–A pale
 turquoise blue wool
6 Bargello I–A light
 turquoise blue perlé
 (two strands)
7 Bargello I–A light
 aquamarine wool
8 Bargello I–A light
 turquoise blue perlé
 (two strands)
9 Bargello I–A medium
 aquamarine wool
10 Bargello I–A dark
 teal blue perlé
11 tent pale blue grey
 SC

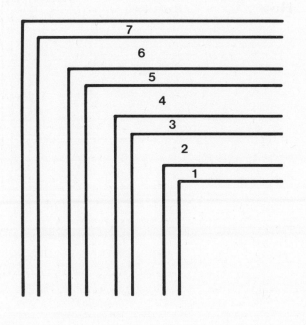

Outer Border

1. tent dark teal blue perlé
2. slanted Gobelin (l to r) light aquamarine wool
3. tent light turquoise blue perlé
4. slanted Gobelin (r to l) medium aquamarine wool
5. tent dark teal blue perlé
6. slanted Gobelin (l to r) dark teal blue perlé
7. tent light aquamarine wool

Inner Panel

work all four sides vertically

all in tent, pattern as in tent stitch detail

1. pale blue SC
2. medium turquoise blue perlé
3. pale blue SC
4. pale turquoise blue wool (two rows to separate pattern)
5. pale blue SC
6. medium turquoise blue perlé
7. pale blue SC
8. background pale turquoise blue wool
9. background pale turquoise blue wool

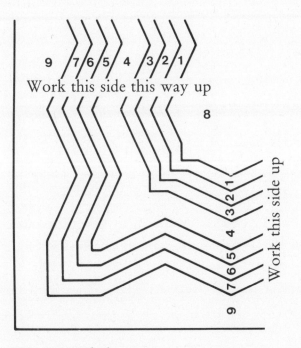

Work this side this way up

Work this side up

SC = stranded cotton

The Blue and Cream Lace Cushion

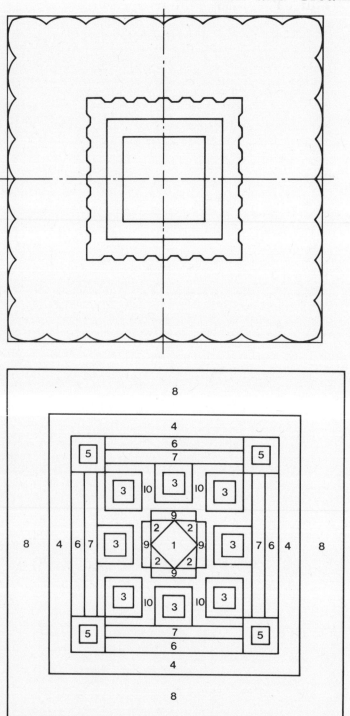

numbers are in working sequence

164

How to mark out a canvas

canvas divided into quarters and central square, scallops counted and marked on canvas

Central Square

1 large diamond eyelet light cream perlé
2 cross light Wedgwood blue perlé
3 small eyelet light cream perlé, surrounded by tent medium Wedgwood blue, surrounded by tent ecru SEC
4 oblong cross stitch medium Wedgwood blue perlé with backstitch ecru SEC
5 small eyelet light cream perlé, surrounded by tent medium Wedgwood blue perlé
6 cross light Wedgwood blue perlé
7 cross alternating light Wedgwood blue perlé and ecru SEC
8 small eyelet light cream perlé surrounded by tent medium Wedgwood blue perlé
9 cross light cream perlé
10 remaining area filled in tent light cream perlé

Outer Border

1 Bargello I–B ecru SEC
2 Bargello I–B dark
  (bright) Wedgwood
  blue perlé
3 Bargello I–B ecru SEC
4 leaf ecru SEC
5 upright Gobelin dark
  (bright) Wedgwood
  blue perlé
background filled in last
in cross

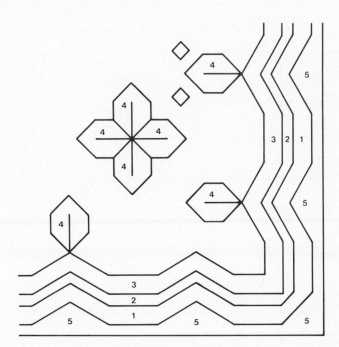

Inner Border

1 Bargello I–C ecru
  SEC
2 Bargello I–C dark
  (bright) Wedgwood
  blue perlé
3 Bargello I–C ecru
  SEC
4 tent ecru SEC
5 cross ecru SEC
6 cross dark (bright)
  Wedgwood blue
  perlé
7 cross ecru SEC
8 leaf ecru SEC
9 cross ecru SEC
10 cross dark (bright)
  Wedgwood blue
  perlé
background filled in last
in cross

SC = stranded cotton
SEC = soft embroidery
cotton

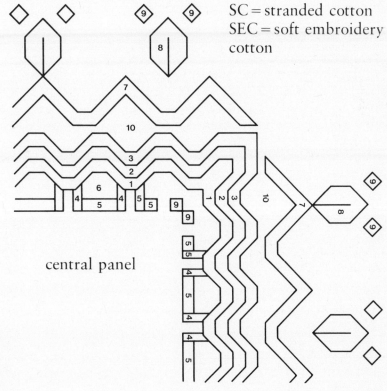

central panel

165

The Iced Pink Moiré Silk Cushion

Border Sequence

1 upright Gobelin pale pink SC
2 tent dark true pink wool
3 cross pale pink SC
4 tent dark raspberry pink perlé
5 double leviathan medium raspberry pink perlé
6 tent dark raspberry pink perlé
7 cross pale pink SC
8 tent dark true pink wool
9 brick pale lemon yellow wool
10 brick light butter yellow wool
11 tent light butter yellow SC
12 cross light green perlé
13 cross medium avocado green wool
a leaf medium raspberry pink perlé
b tent light iced pink wool
c brick light iced pink wool
d brick light butter yellow wool

Central Motif

1 leaf dark raspberry pink perlé
2 leaf medium raspberry pink perlé
3 leaf light raspberry pink perlé
4 leaf pale pink SC
5 cross pale pink SC
6 tent light raspberry pink perlé
7 double leviathan light green perlé
8 tent pale lemon yellow wool
9 tent light butter yellow wool

corners filled in with random Bargello stitches in perlé and SC pinks

Background Sequence

e double leviathan light butter yellow SC
f tent medium raspberry pink perlé
g tent light butter yellow SC
h background brick light iced pink wool

SC = stranded cotton

166

Anabelle's Rose Pink Cushion

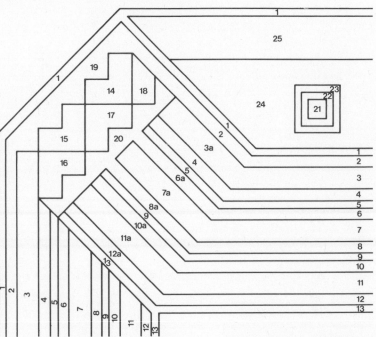

Outer Border

1   tent pale cream/pink SC

2   knitting medium/dark teal blue perlé

3   double leviathan lt turquoise blue perlé

3a double leviathan + tent

4   knitting medium/dark teal blue perlé

5   tent pale cream/pink SC

6   knitting medium raspberry pink perlé

6a tent

7   double leviathan lt fondant pink perlé

7a double leviathan + tent

8   knitting medium raspberry pink perlé

8a tent

9   tent pale cream/pink SC

10 knitting medium/dark teal blue perlé

10a tent

11 double leviathan lt turquoise blue perlé

11a double leviathan + tent

12 knitting medium/dark teal blue perlé

12a tent

13 tent cream/pink SC

14 & 15 double leviathan lt turquoise blue perlé

16–18 double leviathan light fondant pink perlé

19 tent medium/dark teal blue perlé

20 tent medium raspberry pink perlé

21 double leviathan lt turquoise blue perlé

22 tent light duck egg blue wool

23 tent cream/pink SC

24 background brick lt duck egg blue wool

25 two rows brick lt aquamarine wool

Central Panel

1 three rows brick light aquamarine wool

2 letters in medium raspberry pink perlé: turn canvas to work

long parts of letters in slanted Gobelin (l to r over one strand only); work other parts horizontally as usual

3 background tent light fondant pink perlé

4 double leviathan light turquoise blue perlé

5 tent light duck egg blue wool

6 tent cream/pink SC

7 background brick lt aquamarine wool

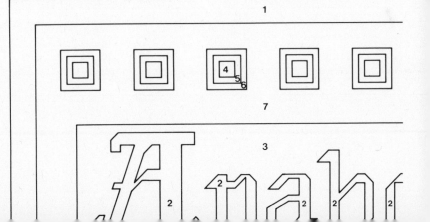

The Lime Green Spanish Rug Cushion

Inner Panels and Borders

1 all grid lines in one row tent medium leaf green perlé

2 all centres in double leviathan pale cream perlé

3 two rows tent medium leaf green perlé (all round)

4 slanted Gobelin (l to r) bright/medium lemon yellow wool (all round)

5 tent light lime green perlé (all round)

6 slanted Gobelin (r to l) bright/medium lemon yellow wool

7 Scottish light lime green perlé

all slanted Gobelin worked over two threads

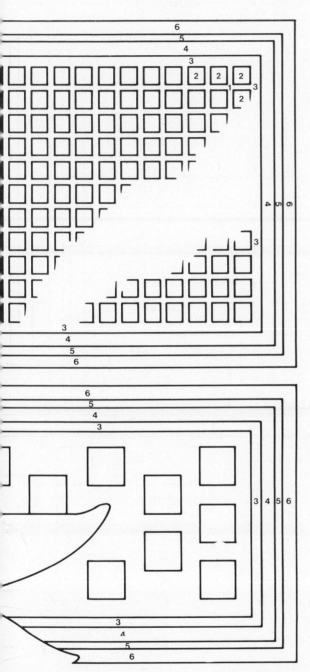

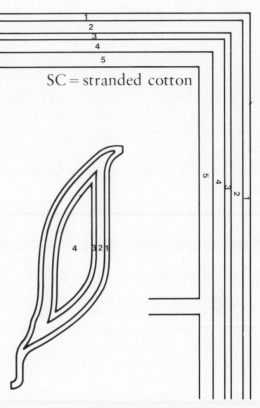

SC = stranded cotton

olive green SC
2 tent dark olive green wool
3 one row tent light lime green perlé
4 tent medium yellow/green wool

Outer Border

1 tent light lime green perlé
2 slanted Gobelin (r to l) bright/medium lemon yellow wool
3 tent light lime green perlé
4 slanted Gobelin (l to r) bright/medium lemon yellow wool
5 Scottish light lime green perlé

Squares in Background

8 double leviathan light cream beige wool
9 tent pale cream perlé
10 tent light cream beige wool

Background (around Squares)

11 brick light cream beige wool

Leaves

1 one row tent dark

169

The Photograph Frame with an Art Nouveau Theme

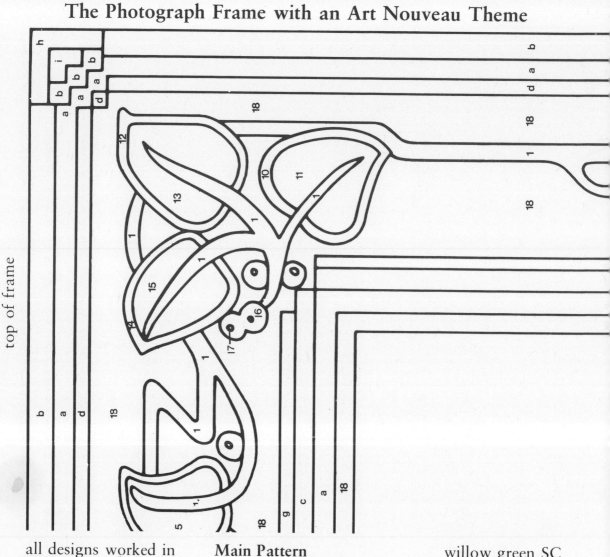

all designs worked in tent except where indicated on borders

Main Pattern

1 all connecting lines and branches in dark forest green SC
2 outline medium willow green SC
3 centre light silver green SC
4 outlines light silver green SC
5 centre medium/dark willow green perlé
6 outline medium willow green SC
7 centre light willow green perlé
8 outline medium willow green SC
9 centre light silver green SC
10 outline medium willow green SC
11 centre light willow green perlé
12 outline light willow green SC

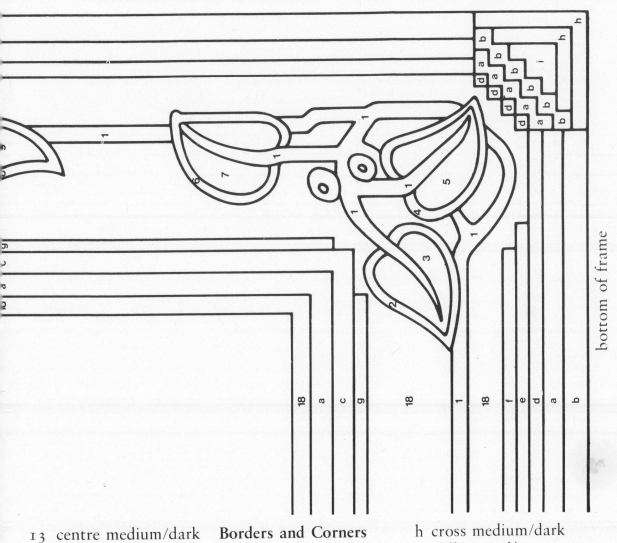

bottom of frame

13 centre medium/dark willow green perlé

14 outline medium willow green SC

15 centre light silver green SC

16 centre light lilac SC

17 outlines medium/dark pink/mauve perlé

18 all background in tent medium blackberry wool

Borders and Corners

a Scottish medium rose SC

b Scottish light willow green perlé

c Scottish light lilac SC

d cross light lilac SC

e cross medium rose SC

f cross light willow green perlé

g cross medium/dark pink/mauve SC

h cross medium/dark willow perlé

i tent light apple green perlé

SC = stranded cotton

171

The Green Initialled Cushion

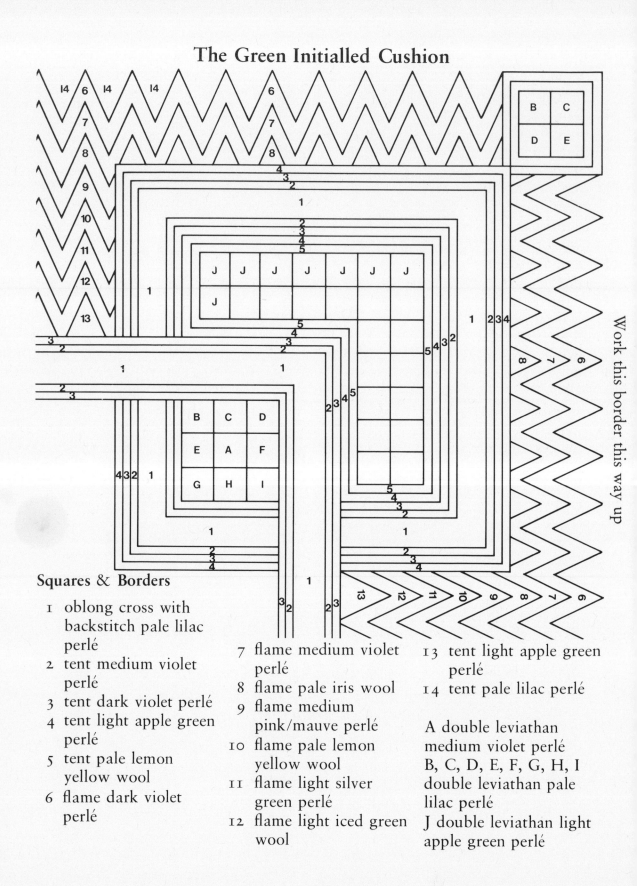

Work this border this way up

Squares & Borders

1. oblong cross with backstitch pale lilac perlé
2. tent medium violet perlé
3. tent dark violet perlé
4. tent light apple green perlé
5. tent pale lemon yellow wool
6. flame dark violet perlé
7. flame medium violet perlé
8. flame pale iris wool
9. flame medium pink/mauve perlé
10. flame pale lemon yellow wool
11. flame light silver green perlé
12. flame light iced green wool
13. tent light apple green perlé
14. tent pale lilac perlé

A double leviathan medium violet perlé
B, C, D, E, F, G, H, I double leviathan pale lilac perlé
J double leviathan light apple green perlé

Central Panel

A flame light cream/yellow SC

B flame light silver green perlé

C flame light iced green wool

D flame light silver green perlé

E flame light iced green wool

F flame medium pink/mauve perlé

G flame pale lemon yellow wool

H flame light silver green perlé

I flame light iced green wool

J tent light apple green perlé

5 background tent pale lemon yellow wool

6 flame light iced green wool

7 flame light silver green perlé

8 flame pale lemon yellow wool

9 flame medium pink/mauve perlé

10 flame light iced green wool

11 flame light silver green perlé

12 flame light apple green perlé

'A' *all* in tent, worked horizontally, perlé

1 pale lilac
2 medium pink/mauve
3 medium violet
4 dark violet

'A' *all* in tent, worked vertically, perlé

a pale lilac
b medium pink/mauve
c medium violet
d dark violet

continue alternating rows of flame light iced green wool and light silver green perlé

SC = stranded cotton

173

The Bargello Cushion

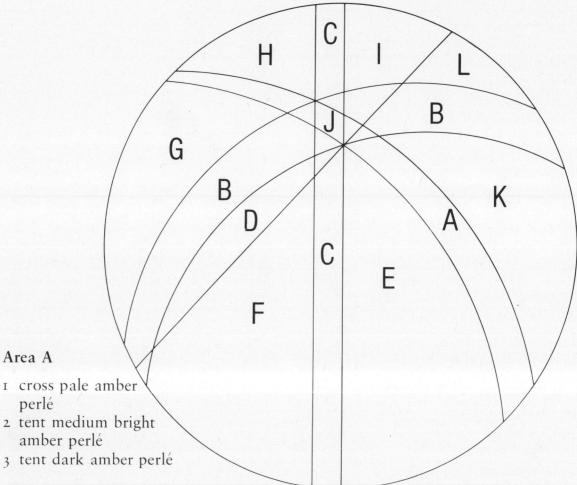

Area A

1 cross pale amber perlé
2 tent medium bright amber perlé
3 tent dark amber perlé

Area C

1 tent medium sherry rose wool
2 slanted Gobelin (l to r) dark rose perlé
3 slanted Gobelin (l to r) light rose perlé
4 slanted Gobelin (l to r) pale amber perlé

Area E

background flame light beige wool

1 flame light beige SC & light cream SC

2 flame medium bright amber perlé & pale amber perlé
3 flame medium sherry rose wool & dark rose perlé
4 flame medium dark blue/green wool & medium (bright) green perlé
5 flame light beige SC & light cream SC
6 flame medium bright amber perlé & pale amber perlé

7 flame medium sherry rose wool & dark rose perlé
8 flame medium dark blue/green wool & medium (bright) green perlé

Area I

1 flame light beige wool
2 flame light cream SC
3 flame light beige wool
4 flame medium amber wool

Area J

J1 & 2 tent medium dark blue/green wool

J3 tent medium sherry rose wool

J4 tent medium blue/green perlé

J5 dark rose perlé

J6 tent pale amber perlé

J7 tent light rose perlé

J8 tent medium sherry rose wool

J9 tent medium (bright) green perlé

Area K

background flame light beige wool

1 flame light cream SC

2 flame medium (bright) green perlé

3 flame medium blue/green wool

4 flame medium blue/green perlé

5 flame medium blue/green wool

6 flame medium (bright) green perlé

7 flame medium blue/green wool

8 flame light cream SC

Area L

1 horizontal brick medium blue/green wool

2 tent medium (bright) green perlé

3 horizontal brick medium amber wool

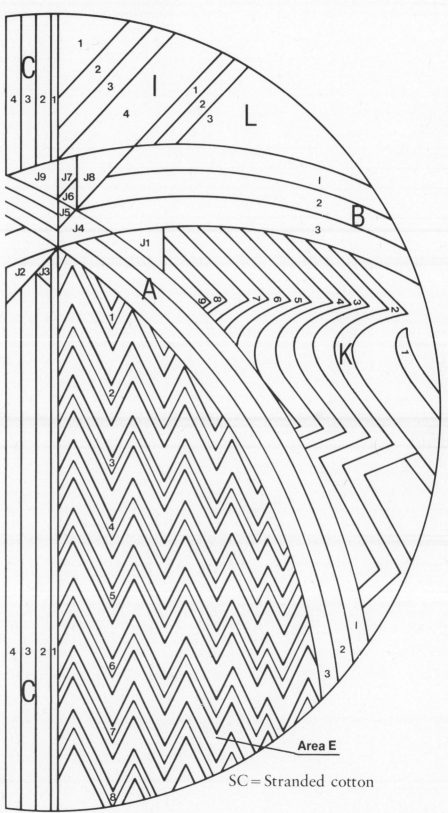

SC = Stranded cotton

175

Area B

1 cross light cream SC
2 cross light beige perlé
3 tent medium beige/brown perlé

Area D

1 horizontal brick medium amber wool
2 horizontal brick medium blue/green wool
3 tent medium blue/green perlé

Area F

1 background flame light beige wool
2 flame light cream SC
3 flame light beige perlé
4 flame medium beige/brown perlé
5 flame medium (bright) green perlé
6 flame medium blue/green wool
7 flame dark rose perlé
8 flame medium sherry rose wool
9 flame medium bright amber perlé
10 flame pale amber perlé

Area G

1 flame light cream SC
2 background flame light beige wool
3 flame medium bright amber perlé
4 flame pale amber perlé
5 flame light cream SC

Area H

1 background flame wool light beige
2 flame dark rose perlé
3 flame light beige perlé
4 flame medium sherry rose wool
5 flame light rose perlé

SC = stranded cotton